REAL GHOST STORIES...That You Haven't He

by The UFO Guy

About Me

I began investigating UFOs and the Paranormal in High School. I started an afterschool club for extra credit which began immensely popular. Almost from Day One people wanted to tell me their stories of encounters with the unexplained. I wasn't really ready for this and it kind of freaked me out, but at the same time I was intriqued. I gathered a small group of students and teachers together and we started investigating some of the claims that came our way.

Although I have held jobs completely unrelated to paranormal investigations, I kept on with it as a hobby and eventually started speaking about it in meetings throughout the USA and Canada. I got the name 'The UFO Guy' because of all the radio interviews I started doing. DJs and Radio Personalities listed me as 'The UFO Guy' on their bulletin boards and online sites as a good guest to have on when it comes to the unexplained.

The cases you will read about in this book are real, as are all the facts surrounding them. They represent what I feel are the most amazing that I have investigated over the past thirty plus years of my paranormal investigations. Read and enjoy them, but never lose sight of the fact that people have many different opinions about what Ghosts are and where they come from. Keep an open mind and you'll enjoy these all the more...

-The UFO Guy, 2012

Chapter One: The Mutiny That Never Ended

Controversy has always surrounded the infamous tale of the HMS Bounty. It's most famous, ill-fated and final voyage began out of England in 1787. Touted as a voyage of scientific importance by the shy British, the reality was that the ship was sailing to Tahiti for the collection of breadfruit saplings. These were to be transported to Jamaica, planted and used as a food source for slaves working on the plantations. After sailing nearly 27,000 miles over ten months, the Bounty arrived in Tahiti. Allowing just enough time for the collection of the saplings, the ship sailed off toward Jamaica on April 4, 1789. What happened next has always and will always be disputed.

After three weeks under sail for Jamaica, first mate Fletcher Christian and those loyal to his cause took control of the Bounty in mutiny against Captain William Bligh. The captain and eighteen sailors still loyal to him were set adrift in a small open boat near the island of Tonga. Allegedly fearing the possibility of cannibals on Tonga, Bligh sailed in another direction. The captain and his supporters survived a 3,600 mile, seven week ocean voyage to the Indonesian island of Timor. After the mutiny, Christian and his men returned to Tahiti to reunite with their native lovers. Sixteen of the twenty-five Mutineers decided to remain there while Christian, eight crew members, their women and a few Tahitian men sailed on in search of a safe haven.

On January 23, 1790, Christian and his crew arrived on the tiny volcanic island of Pitcairn. Almost 1400 miles from Tahiti, the island is just 1 ¾ miles square. Originally sighted by a British Midshipman named Robert Pitcairn in 1767, it was charted incorrectly at a later date and virtually forgotten about by the time the Bounty arrived there. Despite a thorough search for the Mutineers by the British Navy, Christian and his group weren't found. The remainder of the Mutineers who stayed on Tahiti were located and returned to England where a trial lead to seven exonerations and three hangings.

Despite misgivings about Bligh's behavior, the British Admiralty decided that an indictment against him would be an unnecessary blemish on the British Royal Navy. They lauded his accomplishments and seamanship, punished what Mutineers they could and later appointed Bligh the Governor of the New South Wales colony in Australia.

Some say he was merely showing his true colors when the colonists of New South Wales held their own mutiny against Bligh after just three years under his rule. Claiming he was a tyrant and ill-suited for the position of Governor, they arrested Bligh and shipped him back to England. But even after two instances of mutiny, the British Admiralty did not want this nasty man to defame the entire Navy. Again, no punishment was rendered and Bligh was later promoted to the position of Vice Admiral.

By the time an American Whaling ship re-discovered Pitcairn island in 1808, only one Mutineer was left alive. The others had been murdered or committed suicide. The last surviving Mutineer, John Adams, took control of the island and restored civility. With an emphasis on religion and education, he managed to pull together the population of under 100 and restore the dream of a peaceful paradise where people could live a carefree lifestyle. In 1825, a British ship arrived at Pitcairn with an offer of amnesty for Adams and in 1838 the small island became a part of the British Empire.

If would be easy to argue about the mutiny against Bligh for a lifetime. This is simply a case where you had to be there to know what really happened. For over two hundred years it was just assumed that Bligh was a puppet of a Royal Navy known for its inhumanity and brutality, who got what he deserved. The entire purpose of the voyage was to provide food to support the system of slavery in Jamaica, so very few people cared to look into the case too deeply. Regardless of whether Bligh was a brutal captain with a god complex or just a strict leader who was intent on completing a mission being watched closely by the British Admiralty, one can hardly blame the crew of the Bounty for wanting to escape the horrendous onboard conditions of such a long voyage for the paradise and free love lifestyle of Tahiti and the South Pacific islands.

The first time I walked on board an exact replica of the HMS Bounty in 1971, I could easily understand why anyone would want to get off that ship. Despite the fact that it was an ocean going vessel, the ship was nothing like I had expected it to be. It was tiny! My tour of the ship took less then ten minutes even after stopping to watch a small canon fire and reading every informative plaque on the vessel. Inside the ship it was hot and uncomfortable, despite large open windows. In some areas there was barely room to stand up.

Although it wasn't Tahiti, I guess I felt like one of the crew members might have when leaving the discomfort of the ship. The airy pier in Saint Petersburg, Florida, where the HMS Bounty replica had become a welcomed tourist attraction was much preferred to the small deck area and stuffy insides of the ship. The air conditioned gift shop associated with the vessel was even more pleasant. It contained a large selection of books, keepsakes and tourist junk related to the ship's theme. But I wasn't a tourist.

My family moved from New York City to St Pete, Florida, in 1970. The town was surrounded by beaches and featured a number of attractions for visitors who filled the place to overflowing during the tourist season. With a whole summer to endure before high school started up for me again, I took advantage of a generous public transit system and short lines at historical sites throughout my new city of residence.

By 1971, I was in my fifth year of major interest in the paranormal. After winning an essay contest sponsored by a tabloid, I had gained some national notoriety by publicizing some odd communications between NASA and the Apollo Astronauts related to UFO sightings in space and near the Moon. My other major interest was history. I was completely thrilled to learn that I had moved to a town with at least a dozen small historical museums.

As the winter months came and school started up, my forays to local historic sites became less frequent. But the story of an actual Egyptian Mummy being available for close examination at the small historical museum adjacent to the downtown Pier was too much to resist. I headed for the museum on a mild September weekend. Standing right in front of a real mummy and being able to almost touch it was quite an experience for me. But what happened next was no less exciting.

Although most of the tourists walked right past the little museum and up to the Bounty or out to the end of the pier, some took a few minutes to investigate it's small interior. There wasn't much room and everything was packed closely together, but that made it easy to overhear almost any conversation going on in the place. I had arrived on a particularly slow day, so the elderly woman who had volunteered to sell tickets and run the small souvenir counter was catching up on her reading when a male friend walked in. He worked just up the pier at the Bounty and brought a small lunch for both of them to share. Still in awe of the Mummy and reading the story cards placed near it, I didn't really listen to the conversation between the volunteer and her friend until the word GHOST popped into my ear.

I maneuvered around the tightly packed exhibits to get a bit closer to the souvenir counter. Feigning interest in the tourist junk, I listened to the two friends talking. It seemed that a few tourists had noticed some cold spots below deck on the Bounty and asked those in charge why the air conditioning in the rest of the ship's interior wasn't working? At the same time, some workers in the gift shop expressed dismay at arriving to items being found on the floor or moved to locations where they didn't belong. I was intrigued and overcame my less then outgoing nature to ask the two a few questions. As it turned out, the elderly couple were impressed that a young person in those days might be interested in something other then anti-war protests.

It seems that the Bounty replica had more then a slightly odd history. The vessel was built in 1960 at a ship building firm in Nova Scotia from original Admiralty plans used for the real HMS Bounty. It took nine months to complete the ship for the 1962 film version of MUNTINY ON THE BOUNTY, starring Marlon Brando and Trevor Howard. At a staggering cost of $650,000, it became the most expensive movie prop ever built at that time. Like the original ship, the replica was supposed to be burned near Pitcairn island during the last few days of filming. But an expected savior stepped in.

During production, Marlon Brando gained a new respect for the plight of the real HMS Bounty Crew. He made sure that the extremes under which common seaman were forced to live during that period of history came to life on film, but didn't want it to end there. Brando felt that if the ship were exhibited to the public, people might understand how terrible living conditions onboard had been for the Mutineers. These feelings may have come from a place deeper then just Brando's sense of social justice.

During filming, the director and other cast members became concerned about Marlon Brando. He had emerged himself so deeply in the part of Fletcher Christian that it became increasingly harder to tell where Fletcher left off and Marlon began. It was almost as if the spirit of Fletcher Christian had possessed the popular actor.

Rumors flew off the set and into the tabloids that problems with the production were Brando's fault. He was described as difficult to work with and over emotional about the script. But Marlon's concern for historical accuracy took a back seat to his new demand that unless the replica was saved for posterity, he wouldn't finish the film. Despite their objections, MGM Studio executives agreed to save the replica. In return, Marlon would stop creating trouble on the set and finish the film.

Thinking it would probably be a waste of money, MGM reluctantly placed the Bounty on exhibit in Saint Petersburg, Florida. They couldn't have been more wrong. People loved the exhibit and the studio made a small fortune selling movie soundtracks, books and other items to the tourists. But not all the news was good. The replica arrived in St Pete with a history that included some strange events.

Despite meticulous construction and for no apparent reason, the vessel would start to take on water during certain days when filming occurred. At other times, those recording the audio tracks on site complained of strange noises coming from the bowels of the ship. The noises weren't heard until the tapes were played at a later time and resembled muffled, incoherent voices. But the sounds were dismissed as background noise traveling across the water. Since much of the dialogue would be re-recorded later and over dubbed into the film for clarity, this was not really a problem.

Workers who were preparing the Bounty replica for public viewing and boarding after it arrived in St Pete had their own odd stories to tell. Mannequins were placed aboard so that some actual costumes from the film could be exhibited and historically-accurate scenes could be recreated aboard. Those dressing and positioning the mannequins complained that they would arrive in the morning and find much of the previous days work undone with positions being shifted and clothes falling off! It was only after the mannequins had been placed in certain positions that it all stopped. Some of the workers shrugged the whole thing off as someone's idea of a practical joke or guaranteed overtime, but others were less sure. They seemed to feel that a force was at work which wanted the mannequins to be displayed a certain way, or not at all.

My visit to the small Museum near the Bounty replica had yielded paranormal gold, but the best was yet to come. After scribbling a bunch of notes in handwriting that would win any doctor's prescription an award for penmanship, I asked the Bounty worker (who I'll call Chuck) if anything other then the cold spots had recently occurred? He told me it was time for him to go back to work, but if I could stick around until after four o'clock he would fill me in on the rest. I agreed and reluctantly called my parents. They really hated the fact of my interest in the paranormal, but were kindly tolerant since I was an only child. They said to call when I finished and they would pick me up.

After I finished viewing everything in the Museum twice and walked around the area for a while, I headed toward the Bounty. Chuck was standing just outside the gift shop building. He was an older man who had retired to St Pete only to find that golf, shuffleboard and the small pension he received after years of working as a book keeper wasn't making it for him. As a comptroller for the Bounty gift shop he was able to sit around in air conditioning all day, fiddle with some numbers, make a nice retirement wage and visit his friend at the nearby Museum. As I approached, another guy appeared. He was a college graduate in his early twenties who, like so many others who fell victim to the ongoing recession of that day, was unable to find real work and took the reasonably well-paying job of a tour guide on the Bounty. His name was George.

After some quick introductions we walked over to an outdoor food vendor, grabbed some eats and sat down at a nearby picnic table. As the sun began to go down and the pier area filled with people out to enjoy the beautiful Florida sunset, George told me his strange tale. Everyone who had worked at the Bounty for any period of time knew the replica's weird history. It was a right of passage. But George had been there just a short time and was still unfamiliar with those stories when he had his first weird experience.

During the Bounty tour a guide would set off a small, rail-mounted gun (canon) to the delight of the tourists. All the new people got the duty of cleaning the gun and preparing it for use. After being carefully instructed on how to clean, use and fire the gun, George got the cleaning duty. Arriving early in the morning, he started work on the replica weapon. During the cleaning he pointed the barrel in towards the ship. After turning away from the gun for some supplies, he turned back to find the barrel pointing away from the ship. This happened a few times so George checked the mounting hardware. Although it seemed tight enough, he walked over to the gift shop and left word for the exhibit's mechanic.

About thirty minutes later the mechanic was up on deck. George explained the situation and the mechanic said, "Oh, that's just Harry!" George asked, "Who?" It seemed that almost every new tour guide given the duty of cleaning the gun experienced the same phenomena. It would go on for a few days, then inexplicably cease. Rather then get upset about it, the staff figured there was some prankster ghost aboard and nicknamed him Harry. "Try asking Harry to stop," the Mechanic suggested. "He likes it when new guys call him by name." Sure enough, after George asked Harry to give him a break, the gun never turned by itself again. George thought that the whole thing had been a prank on the new guy arranged by the other workers, but went along with it. The next event changed his mind.

Tour guides dressed in period costumes from the time that the famous mutiny took place. The week before I met him and Chuck, George was working around midday when it came time for him to take a break. As he prepared to head off to the gift shop, he saw a very scruffy looking man wearing a costume like his and heading down into lower deck area. He was surprised at the man's appearance, because the costume seemed as dirty as the guy himself. He followed the man and walked down the steps into the bowels of the ship, but found no one there. Had he imagined it all?

Later that day some tourists reported cold spots in the same place where the unkept man had been. Employees had noticed the spots on previous occasions, but in different spots. While all this craziness was going on the gift store problem persisted. Books, tapes, records and souvenirs were still being moved around at night. Those who worked at the replica were first annoyed, but now concerned.

The following Monday was a day off from school due to teacher conferences. I asked Chuck if I might come to see the store early Monday morning and view any objects that had been moved the night before. He agreed, but asked me to keep things quiet. Since St Pete was known as the city with a Church on every street corner, I had no problem with that.

I took an early bus downtown on Monday and walked to the pier. Chuck arrived at a few minutes after eight o'clock and we entered the gift store. In one corner near where some books about the Bounty were kept for display and sale, I saw several items laying on the ground. The same situation was present near the cash register. Maybe it was just that the old pier moved during times when no one was there to notice or some employee thought this was a great way to annoy their boss?

I was still trying to play the skeptic when I noticed something. Several books that were stacked on the register counter were also available for sale on the other side of the room. I asked Chuck if the objects found on the floor or moved around were always found in the same places? He said they were. I asked him how long this had been going on? He said for a couple of months.

A short time later, the gift shop cashier arrived. I asked her how long the book title on the counter and the other side of the room had been available for sale at the store? She told me they started carrying it a couple of months ago. Although I don't recall the exact title, the book was a conspiratorial paperback that told the story of the Bounty from another angle suggesting that Fletcher Christian had planned the Mutiny even before the ship left England. Some sort of weird conflict between the two families became the basis for this convoluted work. But the book was a fast read and cheap enough to be popular with tourists who often purchased paperbacks to read while getting a tan at the pool or beach.

I asked Chuck if he could arrange to shelve the books in the storeroom for a few nights. Seeing where I was coming from and tired of cleaning up the mess every morning, he agreed and figured the manager probably wouldn't notice if it was only for a few days. I suggested they replace it with a paperback that took a more sympathetic view of the Mutineers plight. They did.

The following week I stopped by the Bounty to see Chuck. He had a big smile on his face and dragged me into the gift store. "Here's the kid who solved our little problem!" I was introduced to the Manager of the store and exhibit. Although not totally comfortable with admitting that anything paranormal had happened in the first place, he agreed that my literary suggestion had stopped the overnight mess and damage. Being from Chicago, he had been brought up with enough mid-western ghost stories to at least consider the possibility that something strange had happened. But mostly, he was just happy that his little store was finally at peace. I suggested he not annoy the Mutineers with any more book titles that weren't friendly to their cause. He agreed.

I stayed in touch with Chuck for another year. George found a real job and moved. The cold spots continued, but no more visible manifestations were seen during that time that

I was aware of. The gift shop remained at peace. In my mind, it was obvious that the ghost of one or more Mutineers shared Brando's concern that people not forget how bad things were for everyone who served under the British Naval system in those days. They would probably remain with the replica as long as it was intact to be sure those presenting the history of the Mutiny did so in the Mutineer's favor.

Ships have always had a connection to the paranormal. The abandoned Mary Celeste found drifting with no one on board will always be associated with the mysterious Bermuda Triangle disappearances. The FDR is known as the UFO aircraft carrier because of the number of unusual encounters it's had. The USS Hornet has been called the most haunted ship in the Navy, because of all the deaths and persistent stories of ghosts on board. It has the highest suicide rate of any ship in the military. The Queen Mary has given birth to hundreds of stories involving ghosts and psychic encounters. From a paranormal standpoint, it's possible that shipboard hauntings come about because ghosts tend to associate themselves with people, places or things that gave them the most happiness or controversy while still alive. Such may be the case of Robert Lewis Stevenson.

The author of such literary masterpieces as Treasure Island, Kidnapped and The Strange Case of Dr Jekyll and Mr Hyde spent the last few years of his life in the South Pacific. To get there, Robert Lewis Stevenson chartered a sleek vessel known as the Casco in California. The three months he spent on that ship were said to be some of the happiest times he ever had. While the vessel was being rebuilt at a ship yard a few years back, workman became concerned when tools were moved around and small power failures took place as work on the Casco began. Things got worse when smaller vessels surrounding the scaffolded Casco were found overturned or out of place ruining paint or repair jobs completed the previous day.

Everything came to a head when a tall, gaunt figure was seen moving about the ship in the early evening on various occasions while no one was on board. A worker at the ship yard who was restoring his own small craft was a fan of Stevenson. He knew what the author looked like and pointed out that the descriptions provided by others who saw the figure match that of Stevenson. More importantly, he knew that Stevenson had once been on the ship and that his favorite time for walks on the deck had always been the early evening. After that, the repair job was rapidly completed and the ship sent on it's way. I doubt that anyone was sorry to see it go!

Authors and poets have described our connection to the sea in the beautiful terms. But like every other part of life, the best and worst of things that happen can occur on ships. And for some of us, the consequences of those events may be more eternal then for others.

Chapter Two: The Ghost Of Julie Dodge

It was a warm and quiet October in Saint Petersburg, Florida during 1971. My family had moved there just a year before to escape the hassle, bustle and crime of New York City. Being an only child with two working parents, I knew what it meant to be home for at least a few hours each day by myself. But at thirteen years of age, it didn't scare me. Coming from a city filled with crime and crazies, I automatically walked around the small rented home we had in a nice area of St Pete before going in. I looked for any open windows, unlocked or ajar doors or signs of forced entry. Once I felt comfortable that the house was secure, I entered quickly and immediately locked the door again. It was a kind of ritual and probably seemed silly to the neighbors. They left garage doors wide open most of the day and back doors unlocked until it came time for their kids to come home from school.

Although most people thought of St Pete as a town full of retirees, there was still a significant population of young families and lots of kids. Most of the homes on our block were owned or rented by young couples with children. Although it took some getting used to, I really enjoyed the change that our move to Florida had brought. Even the local Church we attended was a welcome distraction from the cold, closed, cathedral style building where we had worshipped in New York. It was open, airy and bright. And the people just seemed more friendly. Not that New Yorkers aren't friendly. There just scared! When you live in any big city area it's a must to keep a sort of protective distance between yourself, your family and everyone else. You want to be friendly, but you also want to be careful.

It was the third weekend in October of 1971 and the weather was great! I woke extra early that Sunday morning and walked up to the 7-11 that was just two blocks from our house. I loved to surprise my parents with the Sunday Paper and enjoyed buying myself some treats. There's nothing like coke and candy early in the day! But on this morning everyone in the store seemed a bit somber. I shrugged it off and walked back to the house enjoying the fresh morning air. My folks weren't up yet, so I watched some TV. Like most kids, I hated the news. But while flipping channels, I heard something that made me pause.

A thirteen year old girl had been found dead in her home yesterday. Julie Dodge was stabbed to death by an older teen neighbor who became obsessed with her. He waited until her parents went shopping, came over to her house and entered through the unlocked kitchen door. Julie was sitting in the kitchen having a snack when he entered the room. Surprised, but not frightened by him, Julie asked the boy what he wanted? He sat down and started talking with her. They had been neighbors for several years and the boy had done odd jobs for the family on several occasions, so there seemed no reason for Julie to be concerned. But then, the boy started making unwanted advances toward her. She became scared and started screaming.

Neighbors heard Julie's screams through the screen door and called the police. A man working in his garage up the street also heard the screams and ran toward Julie's house. As he approached the kitchen door, the teenage boy ran out and away from the home. A woman who was also walking towards the house saw him run out the door as well. They both recognized the teen as a neighbor. The man and woman looked in through the screen door and were horrified to see Julie's body lying on the kitchen floor in a pool of blood with a large kitchen knife nearby. The police arrived moments later and entered the house. Julie was dead, having been stabbed multiple times by her teenage neighbor.

The boy was apprehended later that day at a friend's house. It seemed that he had a history of odd behavior that his parents had successfully concealed from their neighbors. Problems at school included threats against teachers and damage to school property. On more then one occasion he was seen talking with girls between the ages of twelve and thirteen. He was sixteen. Most of those girls were smart enough to avoid him, but one had complained that he once touched her in an inappropriate way.

Because all this had happened on Saturday afternoon, most people were not aware of it until they watched the Sunday Morning TV News or read Monday's newspaper. There were no special reports or break-ins for local events in those days unless something of national or international importance occurred. If there was a Saturday evening local news report, I doubt anyone watched it. And with the event happening so late in the day, the Dodge murder never even made into Sunday's paper.

I sat stunned while watching the tragedy unfold on TV. There was film of the murder scene, pictures of the suspect being brought to jail and a photo of Julie during happier days. A school picture revealed her to be a beautiful young girl with red hair, freckles and a terrific smile. And I wasn't the only one affected by the murder. Our Pastor spent his entire sermon talking about Julie's death and why bad things can sometimes happen to good people. The entire town went into a state of shock and mourning. How could something like this happen in St Pete?

Things were different after Julie's murder. People starting closing their garages, locking their back doors and became very security minded. It was the only positive thing to come out of any otherwise senseless and tragic death. It took weeks before people started to move past Julie's murder. But even then, the crime had changed things in St Pete. That Halloween was a very muted one. Police spokespeople appeared on TV for days before warning potential trick or treaters to be careful, go out in groups or with their parents.

The only solace that our family could gather from the terrible event was that it had happened way on the other side of town and nowhere near us. Still, it was a different experience for me coming home from school everyday. I was almost ecstatic when my parents agreed to let a nine year neighbor's daughter and eleven year old neighbor's son stay in the house with me after school until their parents got home from work. I was glad to have the company. Thinking as a kid, I figured the bad guys might get one of us, but not all three. That gave us a fighting chance!

A few years earlier, I had become very interested in the paranormal. Not from the standpoint of involvement, but rather as an interest area. Although many books about UFOs, Aliens and various areas of the paranormal were written to take advantage of interest in the subject and had little to contribute in the way of new information or hard facts, there were exceptions. Books by Frank Edwards and John G. Fuller were well-written paranormal case studies injected with as much objectivity and science as possible. By the age of thirteen, I can truthfully say that I had read well over a hundred books on the subject. This gave me a curiosity which later turned my interest into an investigative hobby.

When it came to giving me rides to paranormal seminars, my father usually got the duty. He was a former Air Force Officer who had little to say on the subject and only sat through one of the many seminars that I insisted on attending. I understood how he felt. I started going to these events around the age of eleven, and even at thirteen I must have looked out of place among the crowd of mostly college students and senior citizens. But that didn't lessen my enthusiasm and most of the speakers were more then willing to tolerate a few minutes of conversation with me after the presentation. I learned much from the ghost hunters, parapsychologists, journalists, UFO researchers and authors who gave these talks.

A little more then a month after Julie's murder, I flew back to New York City with my mom. Her father had passed away a few months before and she wanted to spend that Thanksgiving holiday with my Grandmother and some cousins. My dad had to work and couldn't get away. For me, the occasion was a little more somber then I could stomach. We were Scandinavian and they were always big on death and funerals. They actually took pictures! To avoid spending the next few days looking at pictures I've already seen of Grandpa's funeral and watching everyone sit around crying, I linked up with my older cousin and made some plans. As luck would have it, legendary ghost hunter Hans Holtzer was giving a talk in Manhattan on Friday night.

After riding several subway trains and a bus, we arrived at a large hall packed with Holtzer fans and would-be ghost hunters. Hans came out and spoke for an extended period of time about Manhattan ghosts and haunts. I was especially interested in his work with noted Psychics who helped identify and exercise the spirits. It was absolutely fascinating! Most of the ghost or haunting cases were centered around some sort of tragedy. I took it all in and wrote down many notes. By the time I returned to Florida, much of what Holtzer said was still swirling around in my brain.

The all too brief Thanksgiving holiday was over and I was back in school. Mr. Clark was a favorite among students like me. Once a science professor at a prestigious eastern university, Clark had run afoul of his peers and the administration over his spiritual beliefs, which seemed an odd mix of Christianity and Eastern Philosophy. He didn't believe in evolution, but was convinced that reincarnation was possible and likely. Ultimately, he was forced out and ended up teaching junior and senior high school classes in Florida. For some that might have been unseemly and many steps down, but Clark didn't care. He relished the chance to influence young minds.

In his early thirties, Clark could often be found with any number of female intellectuals and hippies in their late teens and early twenties. They just loved his explanations of eastern mysticism. But he was also kind of a kid at heart and seemed to relate well to teens. More then a few of us attended talks he gave after school on various subjects. On the very day I returned to school he announced to his class that there would be such a talk the following afternoon. The subject would be ghosts! It was more then ironic.

The next day about twenty of us gathered from all his classes and attended Clark's thirty minute, after school discussion. It was informative as he gave us his view on the survival of the soul and spirit after death. But something far more interesting happened after the meeting. Eager to tell Clark about my attendance and take on the Holtzer seminar in New York, I stayed around after the discussion ended and almost everyone had left. Before I could speak, a female student stepped forward and asked Clark for some advice. Her name was Jennifer. She had recently transferred to our school from across town.

It's a small world. Jennifer had lived next door to Julie Dodge for some time before her murder and moved just a month prior to the tragedy. The two girls had been close friends and still regularly spoke on the phone right up until the day of Julie's murder.

Shortly after she was killed, Jennifer started having strange dreams about Julie. It was as if Julie was reaching out to her. Then, just before Thanksgiving, Jennifer started feeling cold spots in her home. Florida nights were chilly this time of year, but the family had a modern heater which usually made the home toasty warm. The spots centered around Jennifer's room. One was near her doorway and the other near her bed.

Things came to a head over the Thanksgiving holiday when Jennifer woke up to find herself staring into Julie's face. It was just as real and Julie was smiling just as big as she had on any one of the many sleepovers the girls had enjoyed together. Then she was gone. It had all taken just a matter of seconds. No more incidents had occurred since then, but Jennifer was sure that she felt Julie's presence everywhere in her home.

Mr. Clark thought it was all very interesting, but seemed to hold the opinion that Jennifer was just missing her friend. After all, Julie had never been in the new home that Jennifer moved to. That seemed to go against the norm in days when most haunting cases were poorly investigated and knowledge was limited. I had other ideas.

Instead of speaking with Clark, I left with Jennifer. As we walked out the door, I introduced myself and told her that I thought her ghostly encounter story was fascinating. I enquired about where she lived and found out her house was just a half mile from mine. Like me, she rode her bike to school. Wanting to see what the house looked like, I followed her home with permission. Once at her house, I was about to say goodbye when she invited me in. Her mother was home and seemed happy that Jennifer had made a new friend, even though it was a male one. It turned out that her older sister was the popular one in the family. At sixteen, Christy was a stunning high school beauty. Both girls had long blond hair and great looks, but that's where the similarity ended. While Christy was outgoing and exuded personality, Jennifer was quietly polite, but not shy.

Before I knew it, I was invited to stay for dinner. Her mom gave me a brief tour of the house, which included the area outside of Jenny's room. It did feel very cold for a reasonably-warm afternoon! After clearing the dinner invitation with my parents, I enjoyed a terrific sit down meal with Jenny's family. Her parents couldn't have been nicer people. After dinner, Jenny and I spent about thirty minutes pretending to play Monopoly in a family room off to the side of the house. In reality, we spoke more about Julie. I shared my own feelings about the murder and Jenny told me more about what a great friend and person the murdered girl had been.

Julie was always very popular and had lots of friends, but Jenny was her best friend. The two were opposites when it came to social matters. Julie fit in everywhere with everyone, while Jenny always took a step back and felt like a bit of an outsider. Like me, she enjoyed studying the world of the paranormal. Julie was always kidding her about it, but she did tell Jenny that if anything ever happened to her, she would come back to make sure Jenny was alright. Then, it became so obvious to me.

The reason for Julie's return had to do with the fact that Jenny was slow to make new friends and Julie may have been concerned about her. In more then a few cases, it was unfinished business or an inability to abandon earthly matters that seemed to keep spirits from moving on. Holtzer had talked about a case in New York City where a stable hand had refused to move on and appeared on a regular basis near what was once some old stables in lower Manhattan. Once contacted by a psychic, it seemed he was worried about a beloved horse. Unable to know time as we understand it, the psychic explained to the spirit that time had moved on and he no longer needed to worry about matters that had been a part of his earthly life. After that, the spirit appeared no more.

I didn't know any psychics, but I had a crazy friend named Dennis who wanted to be the next John Lennon, loved Chopin music and had a sister deeply into doing séances. I wondered how we would ever sell this to Jenny's parents? They were nice, but didn't seem like the types to accept the kind of whacked out plan that I had concocted. Then an unusual opportunity presented itself. Jenny's dad was a high degree Mason. An annual dinner was scheduled for just before Christmas and Jenny's parents needed to attend. At the same time, Christy had signed up for a week long trip to the Bahamas with her class and prepaid. There was no way she could cancel.

Since the family had no previous need for a babysitter, they didn't know any. I interjected a thought by telling Jenny's folks about my friend's sister Amber. She could stay with Jenny until her parents returned home from the dinner. I explained that the girl didn't drink or do drugs and was very responsible. Since Amber would be sitting for Jenny, she asked her parents if I could come over and hang out that evening. Amber would drive me home. They agreed.

A week before Christmas, I arrived at Jenny's house with Amber. We said our goodbyes to Jenny's folks and set about contacting Julie. Amber was a pro when it came to séances. She had Jenny take out some items that Julie had given her and began to recite a sort of chant as we sat in a circle in Jenny's bedroom. I'll admit that being a spectator of all things paranormal was far different from being involved. Hearing stories and living one was a totally different experience.

After Amber finished her recitations, she asked Jenny to call for Julie in a very natural way as if she were in the next room. Jenny called out to her several times, and then we waited. It may just have been the atmosphere created by the tension of the moment, but the air seemed filled with electricity. We sat there waiting about ten minutes before a cold breeze seemed to blow by each of us. Then I felt something odd. It was like a warm blanket wrapped around me. We all felt it. Amber said, "Quickly, Jenny, tell Julie that you're alright. She needs to move on. You're happy in your new school and Bill is here as proof that you have already made another good friend in your new school."

Jenny said the words with heart. Another few minutes went by, then Amber announced that we were finished. After straightening things up, we spent the rest of the evening discussing our feelings about the event until Jenny's folks came home. There were no more incidents after that. Jenny and I became very good friends and stayed in contact for years until she died in 1998 of a brain tumor. I visited her a few weeks before she passed on and recall her saying, "Julie is waiting for me and I can't wait to see her again." Sometimes the paranormal just tugs at your heart.

Chapter Three: Can Dogs See Dead People?

"I see dead people." Uttered by actor Haley Joel Osment in M. Night Shyamalan's The Sixth Sense, it has become one of the most famous lines in movie history. Although the film was based on a fictional story, we have all seen those people on television who claim they can see or communicate with the dead. Would it surprise you to learn that dogs may also possess that ability?

One of the oldest known paranormal beliefs is that dogs have the ability to see or communicate with the dead. It would be easy to believe that people have come to that conclusion based on a dog's natural behavior. We've all seen dogs stand still and stare or react to something we were unable to see or hear. However, there may be much more to it then that.

Most of the pet people I have known had some sort of a weird dog story to tell. The most common involves the death of a beloved dog owner. The dog owner would die and it always seems like their pet would know about the event before anyone else. My mother often recounts the story of Grandpa Bill.

For the last few years of his life, Grandpa Bill languished from a terminal illness. When he wasn't in the hospital, he stayed with us. It was during those stays that Bill became very close to an Irish Setter adopted by my mother. Rusty and Bill were inseparable. Whenever he sat in our back yard to get some sun during summer afternoons, Bill would play with her by throwing a ball for Rusty to catch or using her favorite old sock as a pull toy. Rusty slept at the foot of Bill's bed and would start barking anytime he coughed or experienced shallow breathing.

During the final days of his life, Bill was back in the hospital. It was during that time that Rusty started acting strangely. She would pace back and forth in front of the bed in a spare room where Bill slept when he stayed at our home. She would circle the lawn chair he used to sit in when he played with her in the backyard. It was really eerie! However, stranger things were yet to come.

Although we knew he wasn't going to live much longer, it came as a bit of a shock when Bill finally passed on. We thought that he would probably live another few months based on what the doctors said, but that wasn't to be. A nurse checked on him around three in the morning and found he had passed on. Around the same time and without explanation, everyone in our household was awakened by Rusty. She began to howl uncontrollably. Less then an hour later, we received the sad news of Bill's passing by phone.

I was too young to remember most of what happened, but I do recall that my parents were freaked out by the whole event. My mother was a no nonsense kind of person who had no use for anything paranormal, yet she recounted this story several times to me in later years whenever the subject of strange animal behavior would come up. Anything but a story teller, I always felt that she spoke of those events as a way of trying to understand them. I suppose we could just toss it all off to coincidence, but the odds do not seem to be with that considering how many other people have experienced similar events.

Most everyone who has ever lived in any kind of a suburban neighborhood has some sort of a story to tell about that one weird house that everyone would stay away from. In my case, it was about seven houses down from mine in a neighborhood on Long Island. All of the houses on our block had been built in the early 1950s. With slight exceptions of larger or smaller models, most of the homes looked like they belonged together. All except one. The weird house in our neighborhood had a dark wood exterior and was landscaped with small trees instead of bushes and hedges. It stood out and most of the neighbors were not amused.

If it's a true saying that strange houses attract stranger people, you could prove it by the weird house on our block. From the moment they moved in, the first family to live in that house made no attempt to fit into the neighborhood. The parents and three children were weird. They hated to answer their door, had two dogs that were as mean as they were big and never kept up their property.

Within ten years of moving into the house, the family fell apart. After several biting incidents, the dogs were taken away by the police. The older brother died of a drug overdose, the younger one stopped speaking and their sister always seemed to be taking on the role of mom and dad as their parents seemed unable to cope with anything. After their father was hospitalized for alcoholism, mom gave up, sold the house and moved away to parts unknown.

Before anyone could move in, the house was given a major facelift. Gone were the excessive number of trees which had created a haunted mansion look. Gone was the nasty looking wood exterior which gave way to aluminum siding. The inside was gutted and replaced with lighter colors and modern appliances. By the time the new family moved in during the mid 1960s, it was like an entirely different house. However, some of the sorrow from the previous family may have been left behind.

The new family consisted of a couple, a boy and girl under ten, and a cute Yorkshire Terrier they called nappy (short for Napoleon). These people were just the opposite of the previous occupants. They were friendly, took care of their property and got along well with all the neighbors. I knew the children and played with them when they came by my end of the block, but rarely visited their house. Most of what happened next I got from my other friends and people closer to the family then I was.

A couple of my friends were regularly invited to sleepovers at the house. During the sleepovers, Nappy would normally roam the house and eventually settle into his little doggie bed in one corner of the living room. However, on more then a few occasions the friendly little dog exhibited some very unfriendly and odd behavior.

Nappy would bound up the stairs to a finished attic with two bedrooms. This is where the children slept in bedrooms separated by a small hallway. Once there, he would inexplicably start to growl at the room to the right where the boy slept. This was also the room were the older brother from the previous family had once slept and where he had been found dead of a drug overdose.

Their dog's odd behavior was first noticed by the children a few weeks after the new family moved in. Some of my friends who had slept over in the boy's room told me that the boy and his parents were really freaked out by the whole thing. The girl had seen it, but since it wasn't directed at her room, tended to ignore the incidents.

It seems that Nappy got along fine with the children and showed no animosity towards the sleepover guests either. That meant that his nighttime growling behavior was being directed towards an unknown source. I suppose that any number of simple explanations could be used to explain the whole thing away, but the dog's growling wasn't consistent. He didn't do it every night and as often as not slept quietly without the growling when friends of the boy stayed overnight.

About a year after they moved in, the family moved out. This seemed strange considering the investment they had made in the property, but I doubt the reason for their move had anything to do with their dog's odd behavior. There were some strange stories from my friends who spent more time at the house then I did. On a few of the sleepovers they said that the boy's room always seemed very cold, despite a brand new oil burner having been installed in the house before the family moved in.

Like so many other events involving the paranormal, odd animal behavior often gets categorized as explainable even if we do not know the cause. Because dogs cannot talk, we do not know exactly what they are reacting to. Can dogs see dead people? I guess we'll have to wait until we're dead to find out the answer to that question!

Chapter Four: The 'Entity' Case Revisited

During 1974, several researchers working out of UCLA began to investigate one of the most famous and frightening Parapsychology cases ever documented. Often referred to as a violent or extreme haunting, 'The Entity' investigation became famous after the 1981 release of a major film based on that case. Doctors Gaynor and Taff investigated the haunting under the auspices of Thelma Moss, a UCLA Parapsychologist. While the film highlighted the fact that the female victim of the alleged haunting was repeatedly and violently raped, it may have downplayed other events that might have provided an alternative explanation.

The film relied largely on audience imagination to fill in the blanks as the victim was sexually assaulted and highlighted the fact that most people who heard her story tended to initially discount the tale of spirit rape. However, family members, friends and those who bothered to investigate the matter more fully often witnessed the attacks themselves. Some, like her son, were hit, beaten or suffered some degree of bodily harm. The movie seemed to focus on one entity, but the case was far more complicated then that.

In real life, the victim described three entities. Two held her down and the third raped her. Black and blue marks all over her body were clear indications that she had been physically attacked and harmed. This is incredibly significant because it is almost unique in the history of the unexplained. Although there have been instances of everything from bite marks to words carved into flesh on the victims of other supernatural attacks, most of these incidents remain largely suspect when it comes to supernatural causes. 'The Entity' case had more then its fair share of credible witnesses to the rapes and beatings.

Beyond the terrible sexual abuse itself, one event really brought home the uniqueness of this case. During one of their visits to the home of the victim, Gaynor, Taff and others actually saw the figure of a man appear out of thin air. Gaynor gave the following statement to OMNI Magazine in the 1990s: "We saw the head take shape and then the shoulders. The light extended down to the ground until it became a full humanoid figure of greenish-white light. Then it just vanished, almost as if somebody pulled the plug. It didn't fade away. It just vanished. Everybody was completely in awe and silent as we watched this happen."

The appearance of the full-figured apparition always bothered me. It just wasn't something that had ever been successfully documented during a haunting before. That, along with the sexual attacks, just didn't fit into the normal 'ghost' scenario. This wasn't an ethereal figure reenacting an event from their life or some misty spirit. It was a violent and powerful man who had full control over his victim. When asked why she thought it was a ghost that was raping her, the victim told researchers that the man just vanished after the attacks. Based on her descriptions of the perpetrator, he must have been very visible to the victim during the attacks.

Hindsight is 20/20 and I am not going to be the one to second-guess the work of Gaynor and Taff. Even with a good working knowledge of all areas of the unexplained, it would have been hard to consider 'The Entity' case anything more than a very unusual haunting. I'll be the first to admit that what happened in the 1970s would have probably leaded me to the same conclusion if I had been investigating the case at that time. It wasn't until years later that additional events came to my attention, which may provide another possible explanation for "The Entity' attacks.

My first opportunity to speak with several people alleged to have been involved with U.S. Government time travel, mind control and invisibility experiments came in 1988. That first meeting lead to a more in-depth examination of those people in 1989. The 1989 session was videotaped, lasted a full day and included technical experts and specially invited parties from various backgrounds. That session provided enough information for me to establish an on-going investigation of The Philadelphia Experiment, Montauk Project and related events. Those continuing investigations lead to an incident that occurred in 2004.

On February 12, 2004, a woman that I'll refer to as Virginia was joined by her husband and two friends to clean out a small room that existed on the second floor of their newly purchased retirement home in Maryland. The eighty-five year old house needed an interior facelift. With Contractor work set to begin shortly, the four had the task of removing items from a smaller room that was going to become part of a larger open area when everything was completed.

As the small group of people prepared the items for removal, they suddenly felt sick to their stomachs. A green mist appeared in the room accompanied by the form of a man and the odor of over-heated circuitry. He looked like a sailor wearing a long out of date naval uniform. Before anyone could react, the sailor looked at the group and said, "2005. Watch out for 2005! They're playing with your future!" After that, the Sailor faded into the wall and the green mist quickly dissipated. All agreed later that they had heard his voice and everyone heard the same thing. They described the Sailor's voice as deep and full, but sounding a bit muffled.

I believe the warning about 2005 may have referred to the unusually destructive hurricane season that may have been caused by government weather control experiments. While seeking additional funding for weather research and control, a military spokesperson told a congressional committee "The Air Force will own the weather in five years." The weather experiments have a direct connection to some of the technologies discovered and used during various incarnations of The Philadelphia Experiment.

The appearance of the sailor within a green mist is eerily similar to the appearance of the full-figured apparition during 'The Entity' investigation. Another connection is the alleged mental state of many of the sailors who took part in the original Philadelphia Experiment. A number of people who claim to have been involved with the 1940s Navy Project say that attempts to make Navy Vessels invisible lead to severe side effects among the survivors, including mental illness and insanity. And there's more.

Some of the Sailors who survived the original Philadelphia Experiment had a bad habit of fading in and out of their physical environment. Two sailors floated out of the wall of a bar near the Philadelphia Naval Shipyard (according to an article in a local newspaper shortly after the incident).That event was witnessed by shipyard workers, naval personnel and others. A few weeks later, two sailors at the same bar got into a fight. The fight spilled out into the street. Once outside in the light, witnesses described the men involved in the scuffle as being transparent or translucent instead of solid figures made of flesh and bone. They were said to have been a part of the specifically chosen crew placed aboard the as yet to be commissioned battleship escort later know as the USS Eldridge for a sea trial of the P.E. technology.

All this leads us to the inescapable fact that the most famous haunting case of all time might not have involved ghosts at all. It's entirely possible that Survivors of some known or unknown test of Philadelphia Experiment technology could have been the culprits behind 'The Entity' sexual assaults. They may have been victims themselves. Who can say what people who have been exposed to a bizarre technology that leaves them insane, mentally unbalanced and in some horrible ethereal limbo might do?

Anyone investigating the Philadelphia Experiment, Montauk Project and related events knows that you're always at a disadvantage. That's because time is linear and there is no specific database to draw from when it comes to understanding or investigating time travel. If I enter a time machine, travel to three different times in one day and do all sorts of crazy things, no connection to those individual events may actually be made until enough time has passed. As I already pointed out, it took the 1988 and 2004 incidents for me to make any possible connection between 'The Entity' case and The Philadelphia Experiment. It was only after researching those events that I found a way to better understand what might have happened in 1974 during the alleged haunting.

Sadly, the victim of the 1970s 'Entity' attacks has long since disappeared. With a possible connection to the most secret of all government projects, one now wonders whether that disappearance was actually voluntary. Either way, it's unlikely she'll be seen again and that means no additional investigative work can be performed on that case in a meaningful way. However, based on my research into the *Philadelphia Experiment, Montauk Project and related events, I am certain that we haven't seen the last of people appearing in green mists and saying or doing incredible, amazing and possibly criminal things.

Chapter Five: Hanuted Skies: Ghosts of the Eastern Flight 401 Disaster

My experience with the story of Eastern Flight 401 began early in 1973. I flew from Tampa, Florida, to New York City and back several times that year. Most of my close relatives lived in the New York City area. During school breaks, I took the opportunity to combine visits with them with opportunities to attend various paranormal seminars scheduled for that year in the New York Metro area.

At sixteen, I was an experienced traveler and made most of my own airline reservations and arrangements. I hated crowds and loved red eye flights. Traveling at odd hours was no big deal for me. During the middle of Summer Break 1973, I was aboard a Sunday afternoon EAL flight that seemed almost empty. In those days there were always more flight attendants than needed on the off peak hours flights. The younger, less experienced crew members tended to hob knob with passengers. That's how I met Susan. (I am being polite: Flight Attendants were called Stewardesses if they were women and Stewards if they were men in those days)

Her attention was drawn to a book I was reading about Flying Saucers. Like most of the flight attendants that I met during the 1970s, Susan was from the South. She seemed about twenty years old and had a pleasant personality. We talked on and off as her free time allowed. I had enough time in the air to know that there were several topics that you never brought up on a plane. These included UFOs and Airline Crashes, but both subjects came up anyway.

Susan was obviously well read on the UFO subject. Like me, she had relatives in the Air Force. She also knew people that had personally seen UFOs while on commercial flights. Most were not spectacular sightings, but strange enough to cause concern. What really got her started were some of the ghost stories I told. It turned out that hers was much better than mine.

I didn't know much about the Flight 401 Air Disaster except that it involved an Eastern Airlines Passenger Jet which went down in the Florida Everglades about six months before. Personally, I was more concerned about airline hijackers in those days than crashes. Susan asked if I had heard any of the stories about ghosts from that flight appearing to people. I hadn't. Before she could utter another word, a male flight attendant walking by grabbed her by the arm. Both vanished into the First Class section.

After a few minutes the male flight attendant reappeared. Although he worked in First Class, he came up to my seat and asked how I was doing? I said I was fine and didn't need anything. He introduced himself as Bobby and asked if I wanted to move up to First Class. I accepted the invitation. While walking through the curtain that separated the sections, Susan whizzed by me with just a quick smile and stuffed some folded mimeographed papers into my hand. I shoved them into my pocket.

First class was cool. There were only two other passengers there, they seemed drunk and slept most of the flight. Bobby spent a lot of time apologizing for Susan and trying to serve me fine wine. He was either oblivious of my age or didn't care. I didn't drink alcohol, but I did accept the cheese platter and gourmet snacks. He kept saying how unprofessional it was for Susan to upset passengers. I tried explaining that she hadn't upset me, but I saw he was talking at me, not with me and gave up on that. Instead I took a restroom break to read what Susan gave me.

The five folded pages that Susan stuffed into my hand looked like some kind of insider's newsletter. Something a Flight Attendant had put together for other Flight Attendants. It made reference to the 401 crash and how that some flight crews were seeing ghosts from the 401 crash. The pages were badly worn and had obviously been passed around and handled a lot. Although names and specifics were left out, it was obvious that this was a how-to sheet for crew members that wanted to avoid being on planes known for the 401 ghost appearances.

After we landed, I told Bobby that I left something in my seat back in coach. Before he could say anything, I headed back to speak to Susan. She was putting away pillows, so I thanked her for being so nice, pulled the mimeographed sheets out of my pocket and asked her, "Did you see any of the ghosts?" She looked down and thanked me for flying Eastern. Cold! I felt as if I had been dumped by a prom date! I mean, it wasn't like I expected her to give me her telephone number. I just wanted to talk Airline spooks.

While in New York, I went to a library and looked up more information about the crash. It seems that the whole thing began when Flight 401 left Tampa for New York on December 29, 1972. The flight crew was Pilot Bob Loft, First Officer Albert Stockstill and Flight Engineer Don Repo. On the return leg to Miami, a problem developed. While on approach to Miami International at 11:30pm, a landing gear light failed to come on. As a result, the crew attempted to be sure the gear was down.

While trying to remedy the landing gear light issue, it's likely that someone bumped the aircraft control column and deactivated the auto pilot. This caused a slow decent that wasn't noticed by the flight crew until it was too late. Loft and Stockstill perished in the cockpit, although Loft hung on for a while after the crash. Stockstill was thirty-nine and Loft was fifty-five years old. Don Repo, fifty-one years old, initially survived the crash and died a day later in the hospital. In the end, ninety-six of one hundred and sixty-three passengers died.

Two weeks later I flew back to Tampa, Florida. I wondered if it had been sheer luck that caused me to learn about the 401 ghost stories on a flight from Tampa and to New York. Maybe, but I wasn't lucky enough to end up on a flight with Susan again. My off peak flight took off on a late Sunday afternoon with a completely different crew. There were maybe thirty people on board and we ended up with an experienced Flight Attendant. She was kind of bossy, so I sat and read quietly.

At some point, I took out the folded pages that Susan gave me. I tucked them into a notebook I purchased at the airport and had been trying to decode the worn mimeo sheets for days. It proved difficult and was very frustrating, but I thought I would use the flight time back to Florida to try again. While I was using a magnifying glass to try and make out the words and letters, a member of the flight crew passed by. It was the First Officer headed to the back of the aircraft.

I probably wouldn't have noticed him, but he stopped at my seat and looked at the sheets. He asked, "Pardon me, did someone on this flight or at the airport give that to you?" I told him no and made the mistake of saying that I found it in one of the magazines on board. I didn't want to get Susan in trouble. He reached over and grabbed it out of my hands saying it was a scandal sheet passed around by ill-informed employees.

I knew it would do no good to ask for the pages back, so I let it go. I couldn't make most of them out anyway. It was obvious that the First Officer knew what the mimeo sheets were about and wasn't a believer. Or, if he was, he didn't want the stories about ghost sightings on board Eastern flights to fall into the hands of passengers. Either way, the pseudo-pamphlet really upset the guy and clued me into the fact that there was more to this story then a few grapevine rumors.

I had no way of knowing that I was flying Eastern at a time when the Flight 401 ghost sightings were at their high point. The sightings began in January of 1973 and continued in earnest until the summer of 1974. These events were exposed to the world in The Ghost of Flight 401, a book written by John G. Fuller. Fuller is one of my favorite authors. His book, Interrupted Journey chronicled the famous Betty and Barney Hill UFO Abduction Case and there were others like Incident at Exeter that I enjoyed as well.

Fuller's book came out a couple of years after the ghost sightings ended. His wife, Elizabeth, was an Eastern Flight Attendant that helped him get the goods on the 401 ghost sightings. Her book, My Search for the Ghost of Flight 401, was just as good as his and I read both with equal enthusiasm. Anyone interested the paranormal should dig up copies of these and read them cover to cover.

Finally on an economic upswing after slow growth during the 1960s, Eastern Airlines was not very happy about the books. However, there wasn't much they could do to stop them from being published. The movie was a different story. Frank Borman, former Astronaut, Air Force Officer and President of Eastern Airlines, threatened to sue to keep a movie based on the book from being released.

The film, The Ghost of Flight 401, starred Ernest Borgnine and was a part of a one-two punch delivered by Hollywood. The second was the release of Crash, another film about the 401 disaster. This one starred William Shatner. Both films were shown on Broadcast Television in the USA and released in theaters in some other Countries. All told, the films were well received and probably gave Frank Borman more sleepless nights than the ghosts themselves.

That ghost movie brought some reality to the ghostly phenomenon. Most of what people know about Ghosts they get from those ridiculous ghost hunting and scare shows on TV. A few orbs are caught on camera or someone hears the sound of a truck that is engine breaking a few miles away and everyone screams for the Reality TV cameras. Well, I am here to tell you that orbs may be a part of the paranormal, but when you see or experience a ghost, you'll know it!

In the film, the ghosts appear as any human would. For example, during a 1973 flight from Newark to Miami, A Flight Attendant was doing a head count when she noticed a man in an Eastern Airlines Pilot uniform seated with the passengers. He refused to acknowledge her, so she contacted the flight crew. The Captain of that flight came back to see what was going on and recognized the man as Bob Loft. He cried out, "Oh my God, that's Bob Loft!" At that point Loft vanished. Everyone present saw it happen.

During a 1974 flight from San Juan, Puerto Rico to Newark, NJ, the Pilot sees Don Repo sitting in the Flight Engineer's seat. Repo says, "There will never be another crash of an L-1011, we will not allow it." Repo vanishes after speaking. During another sighting, Repo appeared to a Flight Crew member and said he had completed the preflight check.

On another occasion, a Flight Attendant saw a man in a Flight Engineer uniform fixing a microwave oven. Thinking nothing of it, she went about her business. Later she asked the Flight Engineer what was wrong with the microwave. He had no idea what she was talking about. Repo also appeared several times in the Hell Hole (electronics room) beneath the cockpit after crew members heard knocking in that area and went to investigate.

While boarding a flight that would take him from JFK in New York to Miami International in 1973, a Vice President of Eastern Airlines entered the First Class Cabin and saw an Eastern Pilot sitting there. When he got close enough to see his face, it was Bob Loft. Loft vanished before his eyes. Loft was seen by a number of flight crews and spoke occasionally warning about problems or potential problems on board an aircraft.

There were some other types of appearances as well. Flight Attendant Faye Merryweather saw the face of Don Repo staring at her from an oven in the galley of Tri-Star 318. The galley was salvaged from the wreckage of 401. Merryweather summoned two other Flight Attendants. One was a friend of Repo and recognized his face. Repo spoke and said, "Watch out for fire on this airplane." The airliner ended up having engine trouble a short time later on route to Acapulco. After landing, the rest of its flight was cancelled. And it wasn't just flight crews that saw the deceased crew members.

Several Marriott Food Service workers saw a Flight Engineer vanish in the galley of an airliner being stocked for the next flight and refused to continue their work. That flight was delayed for over an hour. Airline cleaners and mechanics began to find reasons to avoid working on or in Ship #318 where most of the sightings took place. Some believe that's because parts were salvaged from the aircraft involved in the 401 crash and transplanted into #318. It's as good as explanation as any.

Although the details remain sketchy and there's a great deal of disagreement about it, the end of the ghost sightings may have had something to do with a psychic intervention of sorts. It's been reported that one or more people who knew Loft and Repo managed to contact them through the help of a psychic medium who persuaded them to move on. The ghost sightings ended about a year and a half after the crash.

Eastern Airlines folded as a company in 1991. Today, there are just around thirty L-1011 aircraft that remain in service of the two hundred and fifty that were built between 1968 and 1984. None of these aircraft are known to contain any salvaged parts from the 401 crash.

A haunting of this intensity and frequency reveals how woefully inadequate our attempts to understand or investigate the paranormal have been. This is especially true of those who do not care to acknowledge paranormal events in the first place. Rather than believe their own people, Eastern chose to ignore the ghost reports and recommend mental health evaluations and treatment for those who saw them. If the ghosts that appeared after the 401 crash have taught us anything, I would hope it is that simply ignoring paranormal events will not make them vanish into thin air.

Chapter Six: When Ghosts Attack, Part One

Anyone that has been involved with hands-on paranormal research for any length of time has probably experienced the physical manifestations of ghostly activity. Whether it's merely a tap on your shoulder or a hard slap on your face, it's something that happens without any easy or sensible explanation. It's also something that you never forget.

As a paranormal researcher that has set UFOs as my primary area of interest, I am used to coming in after the fact. Because of the nature of UFO phenomenon, I am forced to look for evidence that something happened. If it happens again, I am unlikely to be there when it does. That's what makes ghost research a bit more appealing at times.

When someone reports ghostly activity to me, I might get the opportunity to experience the same phenomenon that the witness did if I take on the investigation. In some cases, I may experience more and I am not always ready for it. However, there are no shortcuts and if you want to hang around the paranormal pool, you are going to eventually get wet.

It's my nature to invest a lot of time in most of the interesting and promising paranormal phenomenon cases that come my way. I hate shotgun ghost hunting where debunking is the primary goal and little time is given to the actual investigation. Most of that occurs because many ghost hunters don't understand that ghostly phenomenon probably doesn't exist in the same linear time that they do.

My first experience with a very physical ghost came in 1975. I was contacted by someone that owned an older house in a Michigan suburb. The home was occupied by a family of two adults and five children ages six to seventeen years of age. As usual, there was a catalyst that may have got things started or stepped them up to the next level.

The seventeen year old boy and his fifteen year old sister started playing around with a Ouija Board. Both were obsessed with contacting the spirit of Janis Joplin. Joplin died a few years before of a drug and alcohol overdose. They held several Ouija sessions without any success and decided to include two other friends hoping for better results. Their friends were both sixteen year old teenage girls.

The foursome took the Ouija Board to a small storage room on the third floor of their house. That floor was little more than a finished attic. It had a small bedroom where the older teen boy slept at the eastern end of the house, a long and wide hall just off the stairs and the small storage room at the western end that was sparsely filled with old boxes and disused furniture.

Their first attempt to use the board as a foursome took place in the dead of winter. They managed to get the board to spell out G-U-I-D-E. They assumed that meant that a spirit guide was now in contact with them. Before they could go further, the boy started having terrible pain in his groin area. Then the pain moved to his side and stopped in less than a minute. It was replaced by a very hot feeling on the right side of his body. Upset and worried, the boy hurried down the stairs to the second floor bathroom and examined himself. The mirror revealed a very distinct gash that looked like a burn mark. It was about five inches in length and just above his beltline.

The family contacted me after hearing about another investigation I had been involved with through a family friend. He heard me talking about ghosts during a guest spot on a talk radio show. I arrived at the house less than a week after the first Ouija Board attempt by the foursome. The first thing I discovered was that the boy's sister had also experienced physical phenomenon, but hadn't told anyone.

She found unexplained gashes on her chest and abdomen after the Ouija session, but didn't feel anything at the time. The other two girls involved may have had some physical evidence as well, but decided not to participate in the investigation or any more Ouija sessions. I suggested that the brother and sister reframe from any further Ouija sessions as well and they complied with my request.

I spoke with the family at length and discovered that the house they lived in was once owned by a Master Baker that eventually bought several bakeries in the area during the

1940s and expanded them into successful businesses. He retired in the late 1950s and passed away in the home during the early 1960s when it was sold to the family I was interviewing. The parents of the two teens that had the weird gashes admitted having their own strange experiences in the house.

Both said they saw a figure of a man they believed was the deceased Baker standing near their bed late at night on several occasions. Two of their younger children kept saying that they were being visited by a man in a white uniform. A photo of the baker provided by his widow (she lived in a retirement home nearby) was identified as the man the children saw. When I spoke to his widow and mentioned the gashes on the teenage brother and sister, she mentioned how that he often had small burn marks on his arms and other areas of his body from the baking he did. I also discovered that the Baker died of cancer and became violently ill, throwing up frequently during the final months of his life.

The States of Michigan, Indiana and Ohio are home to some of the most haunted places in the USA. It didn't surprise me to discover a case of this type in that region. What did surprise me was the feeling that I was being pushed around as I walked through the house. It was almost like a gentle shove, but different. I came back to the house on several occasions and felt that something didn't want me there. It wasn't the family. They were friendly, forthcoming with information and welcomed my help.

On my fifth visit, I decided to bring some reinforcements. A Lutheran Pastor that believed in house blessing and exorcism came with me. We weren't in the house for two minutes before he became violently ill and had to excuse himself to use the rest room. Having known him and his family for a while, I knew this was no act. He was physically sick. A few minutes later, he came out of the rest room and showed me his arm. He had a gash that looked like a burn mark on it. I felt lucky that I hadn't yet experienced that phenomenon.

The pastor blessed the house and said several prayers while the family sat around and I observed the entire event. During this time we all felt very uncomfortable. I began to feel physically ill and very stressed. Knowing that I would probably be the next one to throw up, I went outside for some fresh air. I still threw up and felt terribly ill. Fortunately, the feeling didn't last long and I didn't notice any gashes or other physical phenomenon. I went back in and felt relatively comfortable for the rest of the ceremony.

The pastor came back with me and repeated the house blessing several times over the next week until things settled down. There were no more instances of physical phenomenon and neither of us became ill again. However, the family still felt a presence for some time. After a few personal items ended up being moved around from one room to another without explanation, I enlisted the help of several members of a Spiritualist Church located in Detroit. They came out and managed to help neutralize the remainder of the ghostly activity.

Chapter Seven: When Ghosts Attack, Part Two

My next major experience with aggressive ghostly activity took place in Florida. I was in the Orlando area during the mid-1990s when a friend that went to high school with me years before called to ask if I was going to attend a twenty year reunion. We got together and started hanging out. Because I hadn't lived in Florida for a while, Johnny and I barely saw each other over the past decade. We had been close friends in school and were glad to renew our friendship.

Both of us were now married and had children. Johnny loved to watch sports and it was tough to go anywhere with him that didn't involve a stadium. Fortunately, he also enjoyed billiards, bowling and movies which were more to my liking. My wife and I joined Johnny and his wife for many enjoyable evenings at billiards, going to the movies and visiting each at home.

I was busy working with the promotion of several films I have been involved with during that time. Once that settled down, we started going bowling and playing billiards. During that time, Johnny asked if I would speak with his sister. I met her on previous occasions and knew that she had some issues with various ex-boyfriends. Johnny thought that Stacy was bi-polar, but she always seemed to get a clean bill of health from mental health practitioners.

Stacy was doing fine until she hit her junior year in high school. Then she went boy crazy. She always had several boyfriends taking her out, all at the same time. This created lots of confrontations and problems for her family. Johnny stayed clear of the mess because Stacy was always able to take care of herself. She was a kind of pretty tom boy that loved to beat up on her boyfriends if they said or did something she didn't like.

Johnny wanted me to talk with Stacy because she began telling him about strange phenomenon she was experiencing. She lived in a small, one bedroom condo on the first floor in Kissimmee. When Johnny and I dropped by to see her, it was like a reunion.

Stacy was acting like her usual self and nothing seemed strange. She did say that she would wake up and find things moved around, but I assumed that was due to her revolving door-style love life with new people coming and going all the time. She also mentioned hearing strange noises and voices, but I noticed that the walls were not especially thick in her condo.

Nothing Stacy told me during that first meeting gave me the impression that anything paranormal was happening in her life. Johnny laughed and said, "Let's come back next week." I agreed and we returned the following week to find a very disturbing situation. Johnny rang the bell to her condo and Stacy answered. I could hardly believe my eyes.

Stacy's condo was a mess. Things were thrown everywhere and Stacy looked like she had been in a fight. Johnny told me that this happened at least once a week and had been happening every since high school. I was mystified, but tended to believe she was suffering from some psychological disorder.

Johnny didn't say much about Stacy's situation prior to the mess we walked into. I assume that he wanted me to see it for myself. He wasn't a big believer in paranormal phenomenon, but was aware of some of the ghost cases I worked on during my high school days. He knew something was happening with Stacy and had exhausted most of the conventional explanations.

I questioned Stacy about the change she experienced in high school. She told me that it was like waking up one day and finding yourself sharing a body with someone else. I knew that adolescents and teens always seemed particularly vulnerable to ghostly phenomenon and some believe they might actually be a causative factor in the whole thing.

Stacy was always a kind of tomboy, but her new added personality was far more aggressive than she was. It made her feel out of control and came on without warning. Most of what she experienced would be more easily explained from a mental health standpoint, but she had been for all kinds of physical and mental examinations without any specific finding. There were some supernatural aspects.

Johnny was occasionally absent minded. He would misplace things. On the night that he was set to ask his wife to marry him, he misplaced his car keys. He wasn't living at home, but had a friend drop him by his parent's house to see if they had a spare set. He had given his parents a spare set to hold for him. Unfortunately, they were out for the evening and couldn't be reached. Stacy was still living at home and came to the rescue.

Stacy walked into the house while Johnny was there and seeing he was upset, asked what was wrong. He told her about the keys and she tried to help him find the spare set. The spare keys couldn't be located. Stacy developed a headache and went to her room to lie down. While Johnny was still trying to locate the spare keys, Stacy suddenly reappeared in the living room and started yelling at him.

She cursed at Johnny and told him he was an idiot. After a stream of verbal abuse, she suggested that he go back home and check his bathroom floor for the keys. He got a ride home and found his keys on the bathroom floor. On another occasion, he misplaced his wallet. Because he had been to Stacy's condo earlier that evening, he stopped by to see if it was there.

As before, Stacy began suddenly angry and told him that he should look for his wallet at a nearby restaurant. Johnny and his wife went to the eatery earlier that evening, but Stacy didn't know that. When he went to the restaurant and asked about the wallet, the manager said it had been found and turned it over to Johnny.

All of these events could be conventionally explained, but there were some other stories involving Stacy that were a bit harder to ignore. I knew two of her former boyfriends through Johnny. When we talked to them, both admitted to witnessing unexplained phenomenon involving her. One said that she caused him to feel a sensation like scratching on his back when she was sitting across the room. Another said he felt as if he had been kicked in the back of his leg on several occasions while over her place when Stacy wasn't close enough to make contact with him.

After we left Stacy's condo, Johnny admitted that he had experienced some of the same mild attacks that her former boyfriends did. He had been kicked and even hit on the arm when Stacy was around without any physical contact with her. He hadn't told me before because he wanted me to speak with her and the boyfriends first. The most recent incident took place just a few weeks before.

I asked Johnny if he saw Stacy throwing things around her room when she lived at home or her condo. He said that she was always quiet in her room. The only time she became aggressive was when people were around. Some of her girl friends from high school that Johnny knew recalled being on the receiving end of her tirades. None that I met admitted any physical phenomenon, but I sense that at least two were not telling the entire story.

Needless to say, Stacy lost any close female friends she had in her junior year of high school and didn't have any close friends when I visited her. Men seemed more able to deal with her problems than women, and most of those that got involved with her didn't stay involved for very long. This all surprised me because the Stacy I met seemed very nice and well behaved up to that point.

On a later visit to Stacy, I experienced my own phenomenon. Stacy became agitated, although she did not seem at all abusive or angry to me. She was upset and couldn't explain why. After talking with her and Johnny for about thirty minutes, I felt several slight pinches on both my arms. These were distinct and made me feel extremely uncomfortable. I was sitting on a chair away from Stacy and Johnny at the time and no marks were left on either arm. Johnny later told me that he felt something was trying to push him out of his chair as he was getting up when it was time for us to leave.

The next time we went to see Stacy; she had some weird marks on her neck. With extremely fair skin, the marks were obvious to me and I noticed them right away. When I asked Stacy about them, she said that she couldn't account for them. While I still felt that at least some of her behavior might best be explained from a mental health standpoint, there was no doubt that at least some paranormal activity was involved in her life.

I called a Spiritualist Medium that I knew in Cassadaga, Florida. Cassadaga is a town founded by Spiritualists that isn't far from Orlando. She suggested that Stacy come there and meet with her. Although I wasn't able to go with them, Johnny and Stacy did visit the medium. She felt that a physical confrontation with a Relative years before might have been the reason for her present trouble.

Stacy had a cousin named Erin. As children, they attended the same elementary school for several years. Although the families were close, the two girls never got along. Stacy disliked Erin because she felt that her cousin always got more attention than she did during family gatherings. As a result, Stacy constantly taunted Erin at school. Things came to a head and the two ended up in a fight.

Erin was badly beaten by Stacy and needed a number of stitches. Erin's parents decided to place her in another nearby school to keep the two apart. The incident placed a huge strain on the entire family and Stacy wasn't allowed contact with any of her friends for several months. Erin was extremely unhappy in her new school and never forgave Stacy.

While Stacy was in her junior year of High School, Erin was killed in an auto accident. It was at that point that Stacy began having problems. Neither Johnny nor Stacy ever considered this coincidence to be the cause of her problems, but the medium saw Erin around Stacy during their session. I'm not even sure if the medium believed that was all there was to it, but after that session things quieted down.

Stacy offered a profound apology to Erin and visited her grave with flowers on several occasions after the visit to the medium. I visited Stacy a couple of more times until I moved out of the Orlando area and found no further problems apart from her still somewhat bizarre personality quarks. Although Johnny passed away a couple of years ago due to illness, we stayed in touch until his death. He told me that Stacy was doing better and that there had been no paranormal activity in her life since the visit to the medium.

Chapter Eight: Mind Over Matter

During the early 1970s, I had the opportunity to investigate one of the most unusual cases of paranormal activity that I have ever come across. It involved a recently remodeled home in St Petersburg, Florida. A friend that I met in Junior High reported the situation to me. Both of us were now attending the same High School and ran into each other on a regular basis throughout the day.

Although we shared some common interests, the paranormal was not one of them. Toby thought that my interest in UFOs was just crazy. That's why he caught me off guard one day at lunch by asking if ghosts interested me as much as UFOs. I told him that they did. In hushed tones, he told me about some weird stuff that was going on with his family.

Toby's mom died a few years ago after a short bout with cancer. His father, Larry, was devastated and could barely get up in the morning. He lost his job and was living off some money he received from his late wife's life insurance policy. All he did for almost eight months after her death was read the newspaper and watch television. It was during that time that he noticed how many Handyman Specials were available in the real estate section of the paper. It gave him an idea.

Larry started buying distressed homes with the remainder of the life insurance money. His brother, Jonathan, joined him in the new venture. Both men had some experience with painting and carpentry. They were mutual friends with a licensed plumber named Bobby who threw some money and his professional skills into the pot. Together, the three bought, renovated and resold homes in the area. The venture turned out to be very profitable, so they kept at it.

Larry and Jonathan were lucky enough to find an older, one floor house for sale at a bargain price in a very quiet section of St Petersburg. The home was clean, but almost everything in it was out of date and the landscaping needed work. The three friends worked on the house and property for weeks. They painted, put in new carpeting, a new central air conditioning unit, replaced floors and remodeled the bathroom and kitchen.

Once all the work was completed, Larry took on the responsibility of placing the remodeled home on the market. Unlike previous homes that seemed to sell in no time at all, this one was just not moving and the three partners couldn't understand why. The house looked great, the neighborhood was quiet and the market was good. People would look at the house and seem impressed, but wouldn't buy.

Thinking that it seemed too empty, they purchased some inexpensive furniture to give the place a lived-in look. To help things move along, the partners asked Toby's older sister, Maryanne, and her husband, Jeff, to stay there until the place was sold. The young couple had helped them sell two other homes and earned four hundred dollars each time in the process. They were attending a local college, short on money and glad to get a break from staying with relatives for a few weeks. However, lodging in this particular house wouldn't be much of a break.

The house sitting couple had only been in the home for a week when a flood occurred in the bathroom. Assuming it was a leak, they called Toby's dad. Larry came by and looked for the source of the flooding. After turning off the water supply to the house, the water continued flowing on to the bathroom floor from what appeared to be all directions. Just as he was about to call his partner Bobby the plumber, the flooding stopped.

Unable to locate a leak and with no obvious damage to the bathroom or anyplace else in the house, Larry vacuumed up the excess water and decided to leave it at that. This happened on a Monday. He would come back with his brother and Bobby over the weekend to check everything and look for any possible cause of the flooding. However, before the weekend arrived, something else happened.

Maryanne stepped into the shower the next morning and started feeling sick. Within minutes, she became violently ill. She barely made it out of the bathroom before feeling weak and falling to the floor. Jeff heard the ruckus and came to her aid. He drove her to the hospital and waited for news.

Slightly overweight, they tested her for diabetes and considered a number of other possible medical conditions. Everything came back negative and she seemed fine again. Maryanne was released after two days. During the ride home, Jeff told her about an unusual experience he had while she was in the hospital.

Between the incident with Maryanne and rushing to get some assignments completed for school, Jeff was exhausted. Once back home, he quickly fell into a deep sleep. But that didn't last long. Jeff woke up in the middle of the night after hearing a crash. The crash noise was followed by a banging sound that seemed to be coming from the bathroom.

Jeff got up to investigate, but found nothing out of place. All the doors were locked and no one was in the house. He noticed the time on the lighted clock radio next to the bed. It was almost two thirty in the morning. Too tired to worry about it further, Jeff went back to sleep. However, less than ninety minutes later, Jeff woke up again to a loud banging sound again coming from the bathroom.

As he reached the hallway outside of the bathroom, the noise stopped. Not knowing what to think, he wondered if this was a problem with the water pipes and decided to call Larry about it in the morning. He went back to bed and things remained quiet for the rest of the night.

Maryanne was troubled by Jeff's story and didn't know what to think. She had never become suddenly ill before and wondered why everything seemed to center around the bathroom. Maybe her dad and his partners could figure it all out.

Larry, Jonathan and Bobby arrived at the house on Saturday morning ready to troubleshoot the situation. They checked pipes, looked for squirrels or rats in the attic, flushed the toilet a dozen times and ran water in the bathtub to see if any leaks occurred. They found nothing, but Bobby thought of another possibility.

Bathrooms in houses of this type had wall access areas covered with large metal or wooden plates. Once unscrewed, the plates could easily be removed to allow access to points where pipes or electric wiring intersected within the wall. Although they had already removed the two plates where pipes were present and inspected those areas in the bathroom, there were two more located on the other side of the bathroom wall.

Bobby knew that some homeowners had a bad habit of using these open areas in their walls for storage of paint or potentially hazardous liquids. If the liquids started to leak out of their containers, they might cause wall erosion. That would allow any water accumulated from leaky window casements to get out and flood the bathroom floor. Noxious fumes from the same improperly stored liquids could build up inside the walls and be released into the bathroom through wall vents. That might explain Maryanne's sudden illness.

They went to the other room to remove the wall access plates and find out if the previous homeowner had left anything inside the walls. Removal of the first plate revealed nothing but a transformer and some wiring for the doorbell. The second was located close to the outside wall of the house. While they were removing it, the banging sound started and then stopped suddenly. Once open, they found nothing. The three were mystified. Larry and Bobby went around to the side of the house to inspect the outside wall. They saw no cracks or other problems that might account for the noises or flooding.

While all this was going on, Jeff remarked that hearing the banging sounds during the day when he was fully awake reminded him of something. His father was a shooting enthusiast who had taught Jeff how to handle guns. He lost interest in them during his teens and didn't own any, but he recalled the sounds of weapons being fired at shooting ranges. To him, the "banging" noises resembled weapons fire from a distance. With no shooting ranges nearby and the noises being heard in the middle of the night as well as during the day, it seemed an unlikely explanation to the others. The partners left without finding a cause for the unusual occurrences. The house remained quiet until a week and a half later.

Maryanne and Jeff arrived home around one o'clock in the morning from a concert at the Bay Front Center downtown. After the concert, they went out for some burgers at a Big Boy Restaurant with another couple. Maryanne felt strangely uncomfortable during the concert and became suddenly ill at the restaurant. Not wanting to upset the others, she quietly excused herself from the table and went into the rest room to throw up. During the short drive home, she told Jeff what had happened and he mentioned that he wasn't feeling well either. Both were sick to their stomachs.

As they pulled into the driveway, Maryanne noticed a slight glow coming from a hallway window that was directly across from the bathroom. They didn't remember leaving any lights on and hurried in thinking there might be a fire. Once they entered the house, there was a terrible smell like something had died and the couple both became violently ill. The glow was still noticeable and seemed to come from the bathroom. It was a steady, but ethereal light that seemed unnatural and impossible to pin down. The loud banging noise started again and added to the bizarre scene.

Despite being practically bent over in pain, Jeff moved toward the bathroom to find the source of the glow. When he got to the door, he felt a strange fear that kept him from entering or looking inside. Maryanne threw up on the floor in the living room entryway and managed to get to a wall phone in the kitchen. She dialed her father for help. While still on the phone with Larry, the banging stopped and the glow vanished. She told her dad that they were leaving the house, hung up, grabbed a few things and checked into the Howard Johnson's Motel at the beach.

Larry called Jonathan and the two came over to the house around two in the morning to have a look around. Once again, everything was quiet. No lights, no banging noises and no smells. However, while the two men were there by themselves, each heard what sounded like loud voices off in the distance. They went outside to investigate, but the sounds seemed to be coming from inside the house. They locked the place up and left.

I was amazed by the story. Toby became very upset. He wondered if this had something to do with his deceased mother? He wanted answers and I didn't know what to say. I did remind him that most of the reliable books I had read about ghosts and haunted places pointed out that most supernatural phenomenon had some connection to the current or previous owners of the house. That would tend to rule out his mother. Without saying it, I felt this might not be about Ghosts at all. I had read about situations where a force was at work that went well beyond the norm of what we might think of as Ghostly activity. However, checking for ghosts was an easy way to begin the investigation.

I invited two adult members of a local Spiritualist Church to come and interview some of the people involved and see the house for themselves. Janet and Beatrice were two elderly women who had been participants in the Spiritualist movement for many years. I met them at a seminar on ESP just months before. They invited me to visit their Church, so I attended a few services and social events. I looked at it as a chance to learn more about Spiritualism and it certainly was a different experience.

I rode with Janet and Beatrice to the troubled house. Maryanne and Jeff greeted us. They were standing outside and had refused to go back into the house by themselves ever since the incident a week and a half before. Larry and Jonathan arrived around the same time and told us that they had been in the house twice since then, examined everything all over again and still found nothing to account for what the couple experienced. Toby wasn't there.

We all entered the house together. Janet and Beatrice were calm and didn't seem to sense anything. I was cautiously optimistic about their abilities, but hadn't much exposure to the whole Spiritualism thing apart from books and attending their services a few times. They certainly seemed honest and sincere. Both were professional women who worked in the banking industry for many years before their retirement.

After a walk through the house, we sat quietly and listened to the small group explain what had happened in their own words. I took some notes and ran a five-inch reel-to-reel recorder in hopes of getting all the stories right and possibly picking up some EVP (Electronic Voice Phenomenon). Larry and Jonathan were skeptical of our investigation, but something had to account for all this and the business partners were out of ideas.

Janet and Beatrice asked very few questions and simply allowed those present to vent. Being the youngest person there, I sat quietly and took it all in. As Spiritualist Mediums, the two women claimed to have the ability to receive messages from the dead. They could also sense dark forces, but rarely spoke of such things. On that night, they sensed nothing. According to them, this was beyond unusual and almost unprecedented. They later explained to me that it was as if something was jamming their abilities. I had the same result from my attempt to capture any EVP. There wasn't any that I could detect.

The revelations from the Spiritualists and the lack of any EVP fueled my fear that this was not a garden-variety ghost event. It was also possible that the whole thing was some kind of set up. I recalled going to a speech by an experienced paranormal investigator from New England. Ironically, he had been born near Salem and actually lived in what he felt was a haunted house as a child. He reminded the crowd of wannabe ghost chasers that two things would always haunt them more than ghosts:

Over-enthusiasm and fakery. It made me wonder if I was reading more into the events at the house then I should have been.

While I trusted Toby, it was always possible that someone was creating all this hype for his or her own reasons. It wouldn't be the first time that a paranormal investigator had been used as a catalyst to make an unusual occurrence appear to be supernatural in origin. I decided to take a step back and rethink the entire sequence of events. While I was in the process of doing that, I became quite ill. It was like an attack of the flu with real teeth. I couldn't even get out of bed for two days, and then I suddenly felt fine. Was it connected to the house? There was no way to tell.

Janet and Beatrice went back to their Church and sought guidance from the other members. As they considered the matter, several members became ill. Janet eventually ended up in the hospital with symptoms not unlike what Maryanne experienced. Beatrice started having terrible headaches. Was the power of this thing was spreading? Maybe, but I reminded myself that Janet, Beatrice and the majority of Church members were elderly and may have already had preexisting medical problems.

Toby remained on the outside of this situation, but now I needed his help. We got together and canvassed the neighborhood where the house was located. Without being specific, we wondered if the neighbors noticed anything odd about the previous owners or the house. If they asked us why we wanted to know, we just said that Toby was the son of the new owners and they were having problems with the property. Despite our best efforts, none of the people that bothered to answer their doors had any helpful information. Toby's father didn't do any better after calling the previous owners.

According to Larry, the place had an uninteresting history. Built in the early 1960s, it had been owned by a family who moved to Florida from Philadelphia. A couple with two kids lived in the house until their children moved out. Larry had already spoken with the couple on several occasions during the process of purchasing the house. They didn't seem like people with some deep, dark secret. He called them again and asked if they had ever encountered anything strange like the flood or banging noises. They said nothing like that had ever happened while they lived there. The couple had always lacked the funds to modernize the place, but they had kept up the infrastructure with regular repairs and maintenance when it was required.

It was a Saturday, just a month after Toby first told me about the house. I had about given up on solving the mystery of what was happening in that place when I received a call from him. He was breathless. With Maryanne and Jeff out of the house and refusing to return, Toby and his dad stopped by to check on the still unsold property every few days. They arrived at the house that morning to find the entire block filled with police cars.

According to some people standing out in the street, a man who lived in the house next to the one up for sale by the partners had gone berserk. Already known to be a drunk and wife beater, he started shooting at his neighbors with a hunting rifle. A few people mowing their lawns or washing their cars had been hit, but none had life threatening injuries.

The police arrived and just as they were about to move in, he shot himself in the head with a .32 caliper pistol he kept around for self-defense. He died almost instantly. It was later determined that the Shooter was highly intoxicated at the time of the incident and that the shots were random. Fortunately, no one died or was seriously injured as a result of his rampage.

Although big news for about a day and a half, the police tape had been removed from around the house less than two weeks later. The surviving relatives of the Shooter, his estranged wife and two daughters, arrived to settle matters with the property. They quickly moved to clean up and place the house up for sale. After being the victims of his alcoholism for many years, his wife walked out and took the children with her. That happened about two months before the man went berserk.

For a couple of weeks after the shootings, I really didn't know what to think. Larry, Toby and I spent a couple of weekends in the house that they were still trying to sell. There were no noises, floods or unusual activity. The Spiritualists didn't return, but were recovering from whatever it was that had made the ill. Marianne and Jeff decided to get back on the horse that threw them by returning to the house. They did not experience any unusual phenomenon during that time and the property finally sold three weeks later.

Toby's father had been the doubting Thomas of the group all along. He just could not conceive of anything otherworldly causing the problems in that house. Larry wanted to think of his late wife in heaven, not floating around like a vapor. That seemed to be the primary motivation behind his skepticism. At first hostile to my age and the fact that I believed in things related to the paranormal, he changed his mind after I explained to him that I didn't believe this had anything to do with ghosts. The theory I offered him at that time remains my view of what happened I that house today.

Without understanding what really happened, I somehow felt that the neighbor's shooting outburst and suicide were connected to the unusual activity in the house. Three things convinced me of that. First, the problems began in the house owned by the partners just around the time that the dead man's wife and children had left him. Second, the Spiritualists were unable to sense anything because the living, not the dead, had caused the disturbances. Third, the bathroom window faced the shooter's house and was directly opposite the window of the room where he died.

It might be hard for most people to believe that a troubled alcoholic's mental state could have anything to be with the things that happened in that house. That's because science has consistently rejected the idea that people can use their minds to manipulate their environment. It's only been in recent decades that we've learned how governments have used those with the ability to perform Remote Viewing to gather intelligence on their enemies and rivals. However, that's not all they have attempted.

Sometime during the twentieth century the governments of the United States and Soviet Russia became convinced that some people could create a live and accurate mental picture of events happening elsewhere just by using their mind. In some cases, individuals targeted for espionage by remote viewers became unexpectedly ill.

Several American Presidents and other high-ranking government officials suffered from extreme headaches or became suddenly ill after traveling to Russia during the 1980s and 1990s. Experts theorized that microwave radiation being aimed at pre-positioned intelligence gathering devices was the culprit. No one thought to consider the possibility that remote viewers might be the problem.

Once the side effects of Remote Viewing became known, it didn't take those in charge of these secret programs long to figure out that this extra sensory mental highway might have two lanes instead of one. Some Remote Viewers had minds or abilities powerful enough to do more than just gather a mental picture of events happening elsewhere. They were able to enter the minds of their targets. Apart from intelligence gathering, this ability could also be used to mentally harass or even kill people.

Apart from the moral questions that arise from all this, you have to wonder if these kinds of abilities are limited to the conscious level of the mind. It wouldn't be hard to imagine the damage that someone could cause if their unconscious mind could access that kind of power and cause it to act (almost like an emotion) anytime they had strong feelings about something or someone.

Because no one was actually in the home of the Shooter during the weeks before the event, it's impossible to know if any unexplained events were taking place. However, even if nothing had happened in there, it would not be a reason to believe that he had nothing to do with what happened in the home for sale. We must remember that we're not talking about ghosts or a haunting, but rather the possibility of someone with the ability to project thoughts into actions.

The lesson for any paranormal investigator to learn from this bizarre case is that the supernatural, in any form, is nothing to be trifled with. Especially when the scenario doesn't exactly fit into the standard categories. Anyone who wants to perform a thorough investigation of an unexplained event would do well to educate themselves on all the possible explanations. Knowledge is the best protection and most valuable tool any paranormal investigator can have.

Chapter Nine: The Moonville Ghost Tunnel

The Moonville Ghost story begins with the death of a railroad worker over one hundred and forty years ago. According to a regional newspaper article dated 3/31/1859:

"A brakesman on the Marietta & Cincinnati Railroad fell from the cars near Cincinnati Furnace, on last Tuesday March 29, 1859 and was fatally injured, when the wheels passing over and grinding to a shapeless mass the greater part of one of his legs. He was taken on the train to Hamden and Doctors Wolf and Rannells sent for to perform amputation, but the prostration of the vital energies was too great to attempt it. The man is probably dead ere this. The accident resulted from a too free use of liquor."

Railroad workers in trains running on that line started to report seeing a ghostly man who would stand on the tracks and wave a lantern causing the train to stop. He might be in the tunnel, just outside or on the tracks leading to or from the structure. For a time, railroad engineers stopped their trains in case it was a real person warning them of impending danger. But after a while they got so used to the apparition that they ignored it and kept going. An article from the Chillicothe Gazette dated 2/17/1895 states:

"The ghost of Moonville, after an absence of one year, has returned and is again at its old pranks, haunting B&O S-W freight trains and their crews. It appeared Monday night in front of fast freight No. 99 west bound, just eat of the cut which is one half mile the other side of Moonville at the point where Engineer Lawhead lost his life and Engineer Walters was injured. The ghost, attired in a pure white robe, carried a lantern. It had a flowing white beard, its eyes glistened like balls of fire and surrounding it was a halo of twinkling stars. When the train stopped, the ghost stepped off the track and disappeared into the rocks nearby."

People hiking through that area still report seeing the ghost, but it's not the only one they see! The reputation of Moonville has been added to over the years by more events with possible supernatural ramifications.

The railroad didn't leave much room for error when it built the tunnel and four surrounding trestles. The tunnel is just fifty yards long and barely wide enough for the trains that once ran through it on a single track. The trestles were just wide enough for the tracks placed on them and most were long spans. If you happen to be walking on any of the trestles around mid-span when a train came, you would either be hit by the train or have to take a long deadly plunge into a very shallow creek. Numbers vary, but most people who have taken the time to go through area newspapers claim that at least five to ten people were killed in just such a way. The last person killed on one of the trestles was a ten year old girl walking the tracks in 1986 when a CSX train hit her. Shortly after that the line was shut down and more then a few people have seen her ghost!

Hikers that travel along the old track bed and stop for the night to camp out have also reported seeing the ghosts of an older woman who died on a trestle, a prospector, a worker that died in the local mines and one who perished while working at the Hope furnace that still exists in the State Park. But the stand-out spook in all this is still the original Moonville Ghost. Even those who visit the tunnel in broad daylight have reported seeing the apparition standing in dark corners of the structure waving his hideous lantern!

In July of 1977 a B&O freight train was headed west through the Moonville area. Near midnight, an inexperienced engineer saw a man standing on the track and swinging a lantern. Just before he could brake, a conductor told him to ignore the man and wait. He had already been through this many times before. At fifty miles an hour, the lights of the engine shown on the man and flowed through him. The figure then vanished!

New horror stories involving Moonville have joined the old ones. In addition to the original lantern ghost and those of various people killed on or near the tracks; not so ghostly, but equally frightening stories have surfaced of missing hikers, mutilation deaths and teen suicides.

Supposedly, a number of people who were set to hike the old railroad bed through the Moonville area were never seen again. People who sought out the tunnel ghost vanished in the presence of their friends, only to be found days later having been murdered and horribly mutilated. Several Teens are said to have committed suicide in or near the tunnel for no apparent reason. These stories come from the late 1980's and 1990's.

Although I have been unable to substantiate the stories of missing hikers, mutilation murders and teen suicides near the tunnel, the original Moonville Ghost and his spooky friends make up for any horrific exaggerations that might exist in the area. They do have actual histories to back them up and have been seen by enough credible witnesses to be considered real. Ironically, the small nearby cemetery that's no longer used and holds the remains of many of Moonville's residents is probably the least haunted of all the places in that area!

Chapter Ten: The NOON INN - Ghosts, UFOs and Bootleggers

The Noon Inn was built around 1840 and sat near the corner of East Meadow and Prospect Avenues (as these streets are known today) in East Meadow, New York, for over a hundred years. Between 1964 and 1965 the two floor building was moved to Old Bethpage Village Restoration where it joined other historic Long Island buildings in a recreation of life during the 1800's. John H. Noon operated the inn from 1848 until 1859 and became it's best known proprietor. After buying a hotel in Plainedge, Noon moved on and several other owners operated the establishment until 1913.

The Noon Inn had been used as an inn, a small hotel, a private house, a Speakeasy and a tavern. By the 1960's it was merely an unused building that sat on property being used by a small construction firm to store large machinery. The building remained there right up until the Town of Hempstead bought the land for a park and pool project. At that point, the Old Bethpage Village Restoration project moved the Inn to their location. Whether it was donated or purchased is unclear. Veteran's Memorial Park, a outdoor sports complex with large pools and other activities, is located on that spot today.

When it comes to the Noon Inn, we have to ask ourselves which came first, the chicken or the egg? The property comes with a very sorted and unusual history. Although East Meadow was best known for being a good grazing area for farm animals, and later the home of many apple orchards just prior to the post-world war two building boom, its history is sketchy and unreliable.

Two rumors existed about the Noon Inn well into the 1960's before it was moved. It was thought that George Washington once stayed there. This turned out to be a silly notion created by children who attended a school that once sat on the property where the East Meadow Public Library now exists. Most who attended that school agree that the legend was created to annoy teachers who were often unable to confirm or refute the story, being unsure about the actual age of the building. It wasn't until much later that historians were able to verify that the Noon Inn wasn't built until years after Washington's death. However, it should be stated that some form of roadhouse may have existed there at a much earlier date.

Newbridge was a road built over an old Indian Trail that existed at a crossroads of trade routes used by early settlers, Native Americans and traveling merchants. It's likely that travelers going north to south or east to west may have used or crossed the trail. This made it an ideal location for an inn. Always an important crossroads point that is still very busy today, local farmers and apple growers sold their goods there on weekends for years right up through the first half of the twentieth century until the area was built up with houses and a few small businesses.

Another rumor about the Noon Inn concerned smugglers. It was suggested that the original area was a haven for smugglers avoiding British tariffs and later a place where bootleggers moved booze during Prohibition. They used the place as a Speakeasy and distribution center for illegal hooch. According to the rumors and local stories, the few murders that ever took place before and even after the area was built up occurred on or near that property. But that's not all that happened there.

The Town of Hempstead went ahead with their plans to build an outdoor pool and recreation center where the Noon Inn and construction company storage yard had stood. The project was completed quickly and opened in less then two years. On a beautiful summer day in the mid-sixties during the first year of the pool's operation, a huge glowing disc-shaped UFO appeared over the facility. Even though it hovered low over the pool for just a minute, thousands of people saw it.

The object was moved off to the south following Newbridge and was seen all the way to the South Shore until it moved out over the ocean and suddenly sped upwards at a tremendous speed. Flying Saucers had a tendency to follow old or ancient trails, roads and routes when their movements could be tracked by eyewitness accounts or other means. The next day the park was closed because the water had turned an odd color. The entire pool was drained, cleaned and reopened within a week.

Although my family lived just a few blocks from the pool, we were on vacation when the incident happened and didn't return until two days later. I was just around eight years old at the time and probably never would have even heard about it, except for what happened next. While my mom and dad were still off from work and putting all of our vacation stuff away, our doorbell rang. My dad answered the door with me in tow. We were greeted by two men dressed in dark suits who produced government identification. My father later said they were FBI.

The men indicated that they were visiting our neighborhood to reassure residents that what may have been seen over the area a few days ago was a secret project that had gotten loose from Brookhaven National Labs. If we had seen it, they asked us not to talk about it. My father burst out laughing! As a former Air Force Officer, he thought that that was the silliest explanation for a UFO story that he had ever heard. What did they mean got loose? It was like saying that the neighbor's dog got loose from his yard and was found in yours. My father blew the agents off and slammed the door in their faces.

UFO's were not alien to our neighborhood. A number had been seen in the area over the years and well before secret projects were developed or built anywhere on Long Island. Most of the Flying Saucer stories I heard came from law enforcement officers and volunteer firemen. These were credible witnesses and more. Many had once been associated with Mitchell Field, an old Army Air Corps base. They were either working for one of the several aircraft manufacturers on Long Island or had been pilots during World War II or the Korean War. It was hard to discount their stories.

Could it be that the area was one that attracted the supernatural? Despite being a place of rolling meadows with good soil, native Americans seemed to have avoided it except for the trade routes. Anyone that's ever lived there will tell you that the place just feels weird! The general strangeness of the area was added to by stories that the Noon Inn was haunted. During the time when the inn was just an unused building people driving by reported seeing lights going on and off, while hearing loud voices and the kinds of sounds that would come from a tavern or speakeasy.

Since it sat on land owned by a guy named Hoeffner, the Inn was better known as Hoeffner's House. It's shutters were always closed and the building sat unused by 1960. The house was not one of those places far off the road and buried deep in the woods. On the contrary, it sat next store to the local Post Office and a large volume of traffic passed by the structure all day long. But like the haunted mansion at Disney World, it managed to still look wickedly weird right in the middle of everything.

Ghost stories about the place abounded, but according to another suburban legend, no one took them seriously until around 1962. It seems that several teenagers managed to break into the house during summer vacation one night in July. While exploring the old rooms, they moved up the stairs to the second floor. The three boys, aged 13-14, apparently encountered a vagrant who was using the old inn as a place to sleep at night after he had robbed houses during the day. No one knows exactly what happened next, but the three teens ended up stabbed to death.

Their bodies were found a week later by a worker who regularly checked the old building for animals that might wonder in through small holes and get trapped inside. The vagrant was arrested in another town several weeks later and confessed to the murders when the police found some items on him that had belonged to the teens. After that, the Inn became known as the death house among area young people.

By Halloween of the same year, the old building had become a dare point to test the bravery of male teens. Several young people had been arrested trying to break into the place. On Halloween night a group of older teens consisting of two boys and two girls managed to get inside despite additional locks and precautions to keep people out. They began to explore the building while consuming beer and laughing about the reputation of the place.

Once on the second floor, the teens made themselves at home sitting on some old furniture and drinking. After only a few minutes the place became very cold and a feeling of foreboding filled the group. Just as they were preparing to leave, one of the girls in the group spotted what looked like a floating light near one of the walls. When they all turned to look, the light took the shape of three faces. They were the faces of the murdered boys! Rather then waiting for anything else to happen, the group of four ran out of the building.

Although it wasn't a part of their original plan, the teens all told their parents about it. The police were called and checked out the inn. All they found were some beer bottles. There were thoughts about charging the four with trespassing, but it seems the teens were so frightened by the experience that the fear was considered punishment enough. Their story spread and no further attempts were made to break in to the old building. The same night that this happened, the vagrant who had murdered the boys committed suicide in his jail cell by jamming his head up between some pipes near the ceiling until he suffocated. Coincidence or supernatural justice? Surburban legend or true story? Who knows?

Once the Inn was moved to Old Bethpage Village, no further reports of paranormal activities have been reported. Even the strange area where this all happened has been quiet for years. Or it may be that in a more sophisticated time people are just afraid to speak of such things? Either way, the Noon Inn has two legacies. The paranormal one is not discussed on the Bethpage Village Restoration tour!

Chapter Eleven: Robin's Encounter - An Uusual Ghost Story

I was contacted in 2004 by a woman I'll call Robin because she reminds me of someone by that name. After speaking with her on the phone several times, my wife and I met her and her husband at their home in Arizona. In their twenties, the couple had run across my Website after reading an article that I wrote about Ghosts. While I cannot be too specific on the details of her experience for a number of reasons, Robin did ask me to share her story with my readers and Website visitors without revealing her identity.

A year and a half before she contacted me, Robin had been part of a student film project at a university film school in the Southwest USA. Inspired by The Blair Witch Project and Scariest Places On Earth, she wanted to combine the two concepts. Rather than creating a fictional folktale and design a film around it, Robin had the idea of building a film project around people experiencing real and recurring supernatural phenomenon. Hardly a true believer, she approached the project as an interested observer. Along with two other students, Robin wanted to create a film that captured the everyday reality of people who believed they were haunted by ghosts.

While researching possible subjects for the film project, Robin came across some comments posted on a message board regarding an alleged haunted house in a Los Angeles suburb. The posting asked for help or advice. After going back and forth with a couple of postings and several emails, she managed to convince the people involved to invite her over. The three bedroom home was owned by a working couple in their thirties who purchased it in 2000.

From the time they first moved in, weird things happened. A new thermostat for a new central air conditioning unit kept resetting itself down to between sixty and sixty four degrees. Foul smells occasionally occurred in various parts of the home without apparent cause. Dark spots appeared and vanished without warning inside the house. These were areas where, despite the best lighting, it was difficult to see. While all of these things could easily have conventional explanations, they weren't the end of the story.

Just after moving into the home, the new owners noticed that their four year old female cocker spaniel was acting strangely. She always wanted to go out into the back yard. In their previous home, she would go out to take care of her personal business and then bark to get back in. In this home, she stayed out and showed no interest in coming back in until they enticed her with doggie snacks. Without showing any signs of illness, their dog passed away suddenly just five months after moving into the new house. The couple also underwent some changes.

Although they felt the same, people started to perceive the couple differently. Their friends and coworkers kept asking if they were alright, getting enough sleep and eating correctly. Despite no obvious physical changes they could perceive, others said that they looked tired or stressed out. They would stare at a wall or out a window as if daydreaming or distracted by something for up to thirty minutes at a time. It might have gone on longer except for the interruption of a phone call or someone speaking to them. The couple didn't remember doing anything like that. Eventually, their odd behavior subsided.

The couple might have taken all this in stride, but a new and more disturbing element entered the situation about eight months after the couple moved in. Both people began to feel someone brushing up against them when no one was there. It would happen in the house, backyard and garage. The brushing was sporadic and subtle at first, but the incidents increased and became more annoying. The worst part was having it happen while they were in bed. It got to the point where they were woken up at least twice a night.

Thinking there might be a conventional explanation for their problems, the couple spent hundreds of dollars with repair companies in an attempt to locate the source. Nothing was found that could account for what was happening. Likewise, the utility companies came out and found everything to be normal. With few other options available, they decided to post some requests for ideas, suggestions or help on a couple of message boards. Most of the replies were sincere, but not helpful. After a few replies from paranormal investigators, they finally decided to allow a paranormal research group from another state to come and see if they could help.

It was early November and the couple were hoping to get their supernatural problems, if that's what they were, solved by Thanksgiving. It was at that time that Robin contacted them and explained her film project in very honest terms. While they were doubtful about allowing her to use their home in her film project, they did invite her over to witness the paranormal group's investigation and anything strange that might happen. If nothing else, she would gain the experience of visiting an apparently haunted house.

Robin arrived at their home around two o'clock in the afternoon on a Friday. The paranormal group was supposed to have arrived a few hours earlier, but called to say they were delayed. That worked to Robin's advantage as she was able to have a nice conversation with the couple and get the lowdown on what was happening in their home. She took notes and ran through a short list of polite questions. The couple answered them honestly and seemed genuine in their belief about what was happening in the house.

It was now almost four o'clock and still no sign of the paranormal researchers. After an enjoyable lunch courtesy of the couple, they escorted Robin through their home, backyard and garage. Despite their claims, Robin either felt or experienced anything out of the ordinary. In an effort to help fill the time, Robin shared some of her ideas about the film project with the couple. They were intrigued, but concerned about their privacy. To keep things light, she also told them a bit about her experiences in film school and how she tracked down and visited locations where television and motion picture projects were being filmed the summer before.

Just around five o'clock, Robin started to notice something odd. It was a strange odor which she described as 'unpleasant' and 'persistent'. The couple said nothing, so she wondered if they even noticed it? She didn't ask, but Robin became increasingly uneasy with her surroundings. A short while after the odor started she felt something brush up against her leg. With no pets in the house, she wondered if the stories told by the couple were true?

The paranormal investigators finally arrived at the house around 6:30pm. Three men and two women in their twenties came in a van with a phone number and Website address painted on it to report paranormal phenomenon. They wore tee shirts sporting the organization's logo. The couple was taken aback having requested that they arrive quietly and keep a low profile.

The investigators unloaded a ton of video equipment and some tech stuff from their ghost mobile and made their way into the house. Making no apologies for their tardiness, the group began to set things up. The couple had reservations at a nearby motel and planned to abandon their home to the ghost folks for two nights. They hoped to make their two day absence from the house a romantic getaway of sorts, but the late arrival of the investigators had already cost them a dinner reservation.

By seven-thirty, all the equipment was up and running. The investigators were ready to interview the couple, but they seemed annoyed and voiced concerns about being filmed. They understood that the home would be filmed and had given permission for that. However, they had also made it clear before the investigators even decided to come that there were to be no on-camera questions. The couple felt they were not ready for that.

One of the women commented that they had hoped to capture some visual anomalies on camera as they spoke to the couple. One of the men added that investigations like this one were costly. It would help if they could film them and add the video to others being sold to raise funds for their group. However, the couple still preferred not to be filmed at that point. One of the men reluctantly shut off the video cameras and ran a cassette recorder instead. While all this was going on, the strange odor in the home seemed to increase. The couple noticed it and commented. The paranormal investigators said that they noticed it as well, but had no immediate explanation..

By nine o'clock that night the investigators had finished with the couple, walked through the home, taken a number of photos and settled in for a weekend of ghost chasing. The couple headed off to their motel and Robin sat in the living room watching the investigators as they sat at a folding table filled with electronic devices. At that point, the group tried to get Robin out of the house. They kept asking her if she had all she needed and seemed to be oblivious to the fact that she had plans to stay there for most of the night and watch for anything that might happen.

The reason for their attempt to exercise Robin from the premises became obvious about an hour later. Another man and woman arrived at the home. The woman was a psychic and the man identified himself as an observer. Robin later determined that he was a free lance journalist who had showed some interest in writing a story about the investigation at the couple's home. This was something she was sure they would frown on.

The group spent a lot of time filming the psychic who seemed to feel that there were a number of spirits in the home. At times she seemed possessed by the ghosts. Moaning, crying and calling out a number of first names, it was a scene right our of a low budget horror flick. Meanwhile, Robin noticed some unusual darkness in corners of the living room and central hallway. Blinking her eyes repeatedly, she thought maybe it was just eye fatigue from the long day.

Walking over to the hallway, Robin turned on an overhead light, but the area remained unusually dark. She tried pointing this out to the investigators working in one of the nearby rooms. They seemed to feel that if anything strange were going on, the psychic would sense and respond to it. And there were always the cameras. That gave Robin an idea.

She walked over to one of the video monitors on the folding table to take a look at the view from the camera facing the hallway. The view looked normal with no dark area. Looking up, the dark area was plainly visible to the naked eye. One of the investigators sitting at the folding table saw the same thing and tried to get the attention of the others, but they were still in the other room filming the psychic who continued to moan and cry.

"It was a disturbing scene." Robin said, commenting on the paranormal investigators, the over the top behavior being displayed by the psychic and the strange happenings in the house. "I wanted to call someone for help, but I wasn't sure who that would be." she continued. "I promised them (the couple) that I would come alone and I did. They didn't want a houseful of people making all sorts of noise. Privacy was a big thing with them. Neighbors might call the police or complain to the Homeowner's Association."

Robin decided to leave. Things had gotten out of hand and with the psychic crying and moaning, the police were sure to be called as the night wore on. While gathering up her notepad and a few other items she had brought to the house, Robin again felt that strange sensation of something brushing up against her legs. She told one of the ghost chasers that she was leaving and departed.

During the drive home, Robin thought about all the events of the day. She saw great potential in a film about the house despite the circus atmosphere created by the ghost folks, but was sure that the couple would never agree to it. Besides, the events at the house had been far more pronounced than she had expected and Robin wondered if she would be able to deal with it all? Once home, she fell asleep quickly and slept until late morning the next day.

Robin spent most of Saturday afternoon calling the others that were to be a part of the film project. They were amazed at her report, but skeptical regarding all the goings on at the couple's home. The students met later that day to discuss the project further. Whether the events at the house were caused by the supernatural or not, the others decided that the prospects for a film like that were just too good to ignore. They urged Robin to contact the couple again and try to persuade them to cooperate with the film project.

Robin was staying at her Aunt's home to save money on school expenses. Her Aunt lived close to the school, was single and had two spare rooms in her home. The rooms were set apart from the rest of the house and had their own shared kitchen and bathroom. She rented these to students year round. The extra money paid the mortgage and helped with the upkeep on her home. Robin occupied one of the rooms while another girl rented the other. Her Aunt refused to take any money from her and she appreciated the generosity.

Still exhausted from her experience on Friday, Robin was glad she had a light weekend ahead. She worked on a few papers that were coming due and did some reading. Sometime late on Saturday night, Robin began to notice that the room seemed to darken a bit from time to time. This had happened before whenever her Aunt was vacuuming or running the washer and dryer at the same time. But it was late at night and she heard no sounds coming from the other side of the house that might indicate anyone was using the vacuum or any other power hungry appliances.

Robin knocked on the door of the other girl renting from her Aunt. She wanted to see if the same thing was happening in her room, but the girl wasn't home. Back in her room, she was certain that her imagination was simply getting the best of her. She came from a very normal background and had a stable family life as a child. She admitted that it didn't take much to rattle her. The events of the past few days had certainly been more than enough to do that. Robin fell asleep.

Robin called the couple late on Sunday morning. They weren't at the hotel, so she tried the house. They were back home. As she had predicted, a neighbor had called the police because of all the noise coming from the home on Friday night. After confronting the paranormal investigators at the house, the police contacted the couple. Angry and disappointed, they kicked the ghost chasers and their friends out of the house.

Despite the problems with the investigators, the couple had no problems with Robin and asked her back the following weekend. All during that week Robin felt a sense of dread, but thought it might just have been a reaction to the problems caused by the ghost investigators. She wanted to face her fears and visit the couple, so she put the odd feelings out of her mind.

She arrived at the couple's house in the late afternoon. Explaining that her partners wanted her to discuss their film school project with them further, she had a few ideas how a film might be made about their house without revealing their identity of the location of their property. Feeling a bit guilty because she couldn't offer any explanation for their situation or resolution to their problem, Robin offered to contact several professors at her university that had an interest in the paranormal. They might be able to help.

While the three chatted, Robin again noticed the foul odor and began to feel very uncomfortable. Twice she felt something rub up against her arms. It was enough. She excused herself and left. All during the drive home she felt frightened and sick. She realized that going back to the house had been a mistake. Whether it was all in her head or actually happening, Robin knew that she was not prepared for this kind of thing. After returning home, she felt better. However, it was a few weeks before she was able to shake the feeling of dread. During that time she felt as though something was watching her constantly.

Robin convinced her film school project partners to go in a completely different direction, but she was unable to complete the project with them. Back at her parents home in Arizona for the Christmas Holiday, she decided to take a break from school. The pressure of student life, along with the events at the house, had been too much for her. She took a part time job and got reacquainted with someone she had dated for several years.

The decision may have been a bad one academically speaking, but it was good for Robin in the long run. She and her boyfriend were married that spring. Robin helped her husband run his successful business and the two seemed very happy when my wife and I met them. Despite putting the events at the house behind her, Robin wanted people to know what had happened and get some help for the couple.

After reading an article that I wrote about paranormal investigation methods, she visited my Website and contacted me. She was looking for some help for the couple. However, when we contacted them, they had sold the troubled house and moved on. The new owners hadn't contacted them about any disturbances, so it seems the incidents had come to an end. The couple told us that nothing unusual had happened to them since the move.

Robin has a message for my readers: "Since the events at the house I have met Bill and a couple of other paranormal researchers that have helped me get past what happened. The researchers that came to the couple's home really upset me. It's comforting to know that not everyone involved in paranormal research behaves the way they did. I still not sure if what happened had anything to do with something supernatural. I am sure that no one would want to feel the way I did during those experiences. Be careful.

Epilogue

Thank you for joining me on this journey through the unknown. To view more books like this one, please visit http://jsi4.tripod.com/js/storejs.html

Books available:

The History Of Ghosts and Vampires

THE DARK MASTER

UFOs: Government Secrets Kept

The TRUTH About The PHILADELPHIA EXPERIMENT

Printed in Great Britain
by Amazon.co.uk, Ltd.,
Marston Gate.